SPEAKING ILL OF THE DEAD:

Jerks in Chicago History

Adam Selzer

Guilford, Connecticut

Dedicated to the guy who gave me my last
parking ticket—the only living jerk in this book.

To buy books in quantity for corporate use
or incentives, call **(800) 962-0973**
or e-mail **premiums@GlobePequot.com.**

Copyright © 2012 by Morris Book Publishing, LLC

Text design: Sheryl P. Kober
Project editor: Lauren Brancato
Layout artist: Justin Marciano

Library of Congress Cataloging-in-Publication Data

Selzer, Adam.
 Speaking ill of the dead : jerks in Chicago history / Adam Selzer.
    p. cm.
 ISBN 978-0-7627-7291-9
 1. Chicago (Ill.)—History—Anecdotes. 2. Chicago
(Ill.)—Biography—Anecdotes. 3.
Outlaws—Illinois—Chicago—Biography—Anecdotes. 4. Rogues and
vagabonds—Illinois—Chicago—Biography—Anecdotes. 5.
Criminals—Illinois—Chicago—Biography—Anecdotes. I. Title. II.
Title: Jerks in chicago history.
 F548.36.S45 2012
 977.3'110099—dc23

                                                                    2012028625

Printed in the United States of America

10 9 8 7 6 5 4 3 2 1

Contents

CONTENTS

Acknowledgments

Thanks to all the people I've met and worked with in my years of digging into Chicago's history, including Scotti Cohn, Hector Reyes, Willie Williams, Wendy Weaver, Ken Scholes, Dave Cowan, Ursula Bielski, Troy Taylor, Ray Johnson, James Card, Jeff Mudgett, Robert Loerzel, and all of the guys down at the hardware store on Grand Avenue.

Introduction

Everywhere I go in Chicago, people are friendly. My neighbors wave at me as I walk by, and I can't take a stroll to the bank and back without seeing five or six people I know. Now and then I've seen entire crowds at train stations sing along with the Beatles tune a busker is singing. I get into long conversations with total strangers at the diner. I never got anything like this sense of community when I lived in small towns; this is definitely not the same city I saw in *Adventures in Babysitting* in the 1980s.

And yet, Chicago has always been known for its jerks. Chicago politicians are synonymous with corruption, the police are synonymous with brutality, and for such a young city, we've had a pretty alarming number of psychopaths and serial killers over the years.

But from those douchebags who keep having drunken bean-bag-tossing matches outside my window at 2:00 a.m. to the guy who gave me a ticket after the city towed my car into the "no parking" zone when they re-paved my street, it is a city full of jerks. Get a few million people into one town, and you're bound to get a few of those.

But when they're not killing you, robbing you, or writing you a ticket, those jerks can start to seem like colorful characters. In their own odd way, some of the biggest dead jerks in local history have helped make Chicago the wonderful city that it is today. Sometimes they give us all something to talk about, sometimes they teach us valuable lessons, and sometimes they can be just plain entertaining.

Or, at the very least, they give us easy targets when we want to make fun of someone. There's no reason to feel guilty for making fun of thugs, killers, ne'er-do-wells, or jackasses.

Like these ones.

CHAPTER I

John Kinzie
Founding Father, Brawler, and Killer

Chicago is a young city—the oldest houses standing in town date only to the mid-1830s. There are none of the eighteenth-century graveyards one sees in New York City, or the seventeenth-century farm houses of New England. It was only in the late eighteenth century that a single non-native settler, Jean Baptiste Pont DuSable, moved to the area. In those days, "Chicago" was just a mudhole by the river that the local Potowatomie Indians thought smelled bad.

Some have called DuSable "the founder of Chicago," but, in reality, he was just the first non-native settler to live in the vicinity. Where he came from and what brought him to the area where the Chicago River extends out of Lake Michigan are not really known—one theory is that he was a pirate on the run from the lawmakers who were after him in the Caribbean.

Little is known of DuSable's life at all, really, but in the earliest-known references to him, he is referred to as a handsome, well-educated man who settled in "Eschecagou." On a couple of occasions in the 1770s he was arrested on the suspicion of being an American sympathizer (which was still illegal at the time), but despite these problems, and whatever had happened to him in the past, by the late 1780s he was regarded as wealthy and living about as well as a person could on the edge of the wilderness. He owned a spacious log cabin filled with paintings and fine furniture. Also on his property stood a couple of barns, a mill, a chicken coop, and a dairy. The lakefront property wasn't nearly as good a location in terms of property values as it would become in the future, but our "first citizen" certainly seems to have done well for himself.

In 1790, he sold his property to a man who later generations would be taught was the true "founder" of Chicago, one John Kinzie. For generations, Kinzie was thought of as a hero—partly because most of what we knew about him came from books written about him by his daughter-in-law, who, it is fair to say, was a little on the fawning side, even though, in fact, she never met him; she wrote the book because she thought that being married to the son of the founder of Chicago would give her a boost in social circles. Perhaps it's just "dead-white-male bashing," but more recent studies have generally supported the view that John Kinzie was not so much Chicago's founder as Chicago's first notable jerk.

Kinzie began his own career by running away from home. Born in Quebec and raised largely by a stepfather in New York, John Kinzie first fled from his parents—and the country—at the age of ten. While his frantic family searched around, eventually concluding that he must have drowned and been washed out to sea, the little rapscallion had, in fact, decided to look for his father's relatives back in Quebec and stowed away on a boat on the Hudson.

He had no luck in finding any family members, as far as we know, and wound up taking a job with a silversmith—the sort of thing you could still do in those days before child labor laws came into effect. He stayed in Quebec for three years, until the day when his devastated family learned of his whereabouts and brought him back to New York.

The wanderlust stayed with him, though, and he determined to make a career for himself as an Indian trader. Like so many young men of his generation, he decided to go west and grow up with his country.

Kinzie came to Chicago in 1804 and established himself as a fur trader and Indian interpreter who helped the local tribes deal with the settlers at Fort Dearborn, Chicago's first permanent settlement, which stood near the present-day site of Wacker Drive and Michigan Avenue.

The Kinzie "Mansion" as it appeared in 1832.
LaLime's grave was not far away.
ILLINOIS STATE LIBRARY

It's difficult to overstate just how remote Chicago truly was at the time. Not exactly a city of its own yet, by any real definition of the word, Chicago stood that the edge of a largely unsettled country, a wilderness so dark it scared soldiers out of their wits. Business for trading posts was limited, to say the least. As for the village itself, one traveler described it as "(a) few huts, inhabited by a miserable race of men, scarcely equal to the Indians from whom they are descended. Their log or bark houses are low, filthy, and disgusting." This, perhaps, could go down in history as the first time a suburbanite sneered at the city.

Naturally, in such an environment, with few traders traveling through, competition for business among the few businessmen in town was fierce. While Kinzie established himself as a fur trader, DuSable's own house was being inhabited by one Jean LaLime, who had bought it from DuSable for a little over six thousand bucks—a huge sum at the time—around the year 1800. By some accounts, Kinzie had made a better offer, but DuSable couldn't stand the thought of as big a jerk as Kinzie taking over his property. By other accounts, Kinzie had never met DuSable—he certainly hadn't settled in Chicago as of 1800.

In any case, Kinzie bought it from LaLime, probably for far less than he'd paid for it, in 1804.

Kinzie had, by this time, established himself as the most prominent citizen in town, having amassed a good deal of money dealing in fur, trinkets, and, allegedly, slaves. Though his conduct was supposed to be governed by the settlers at Fort Dearborn, he owned a few slaves (which was grossly illegal in Illinois) and sold liquor to the Potowatomi in direct violation of orders from the captain of the fort, Captain John Whistler. Kinzie dealt with these regulations by getting Whistler fired.

Even after Kinzie moved into LaLime's house, LaLime stayed in the area, working as an interpreter. As Kinzie himself began to do more interpreting work, LaLime began to feel that Kinzie was trying to muscle into his territory. The fights between the two got rough, and ended in April of 1812, when Kinzie stabbed LaLime to death and fled to Milwaukee. He returned after a military tribunal ruled that he had acted in self-defense—which may or may not have truly been the case.

The official version of the story has always been that LaLime started the fight by shooting Kinzie in the shoulder, but there's really no reason to believe it's true. A more plausible story is that Kinzie simply stabbed LaLime to death during a brawl, and the settlers at the fort went along with the "self-defense" verdict to spare themselves the trouble of hanging Kinzie. Some speculate they wanted to get rid of LaLime anyway, on the grounds that he had been informing their superiors of corruption within the fort. Certainly the idea that Kinzie brought a knife to a gunfight and won is hard to believe, as is the idea that he was still able to chase LaLime down and stab him after being shot in the shoulder. In movies, guys who are shot in the shoulder can usually just "walk off" the pain in a few steps. In reality, few men who are shot in the shoulder are able to get right up and start stabbing people, even with their non-shot arm.

But in the remote outposts of the early nineteenth century, covering up a murder wasn't a difficult task.

Meanwhile, though, the War of 1812 was in full bloom, and Fort Dearborn was targeted by the British. The settlers were massacred by the Potowatomi, and Kinzie barely escaped with his life, returning to the area in 1816 when things had settled down.

By then, though, the area wasn't as wild and open as it had once been, and Kinzie lived the last decade of his life as a simple employee of a large fur company. It was only decades later that his social-climbing daughter-in-law began to promote him as the "Founder of Chicago."

Some historians have been willing to go along with her account, but others have simply described Kinzie as a "hard drinking village brawler" who became important enough to have a street named after him merely by being in town before most other people were.

After his death he was buried four times: First, in the Fort Dearborn Cemetery near the fort itself; then, when an early cemetery was established near the present-day site of Chicago Avenue and Clark Street, the body was moved there. When *that* one was closed and the official Chicago City Cemetery (now Lincoln Park) opened, he was moved again. But City Cemetery, too, turned out to be a temporary place; it was closed in the 1860s and Kinzie's tombstone was moved to Graceland Cemetery, where it stands today.

But a lot of the bodies were left behind when the cemeteries were moved (workers digging in grounds where they once stood routinely uncover some gruesome surprises), and whether Kinzie's remains truly made the trip every time, or if they're now rotting away somewhere in the middle of Lincoln Park, will remain a matter of guesswork unless some enterprising historian with a shovel and a flashlight makes a midnight run to Graceland one day.

CHAPTER 2

Harper the Drunk and
Stone the Killer
A Lush to the Last,
The First to be Hanged

In 1837 the settlement officially incorporated as a city. The last of the Native American tribes were sent west a couple of years later, and the city began a period of wild growth as speculators came in to snap up land. The city made the slow transition from being a little mudhole on the prairie to being a big mudhole on the prairie.

But it was still muddy, all right. Carriages were often seen stuck and sinking in the ubiquitous sludge, and pranksters would put up signs pointing downward reading "Shortest Road to China."

One of the most fascinating characters who dwelled in the city in those days was George White, more commonly called "Black George," who was the town crier. He would roam the streets, sometimes on horseback, announcing auctions, lost children, and other news. Judge Canton, an early citizen, remembered White as "a stout, very black Negro, with a voice which might have answered in place of a fog whistle . . . his voice could be heard from Wolf Point [the space where the river branches meet near Wacker and Lake] to Fort Dearborn [at Wacker and Michigan]."

With his partner, "Black Pete," White seems to have functioned in any number capacities as a local jack of all trades. Merchants would hire George and Pete to sing outside of their establishments to drum up business. "The town criers were both star performers," remembered early settler Edwin Oscar Gale, "and gave a better show than a negro minstrelsy with a new program every night. As a rule they treated us to rolling songs, bubbling with merriment, in the plantation dialect."

By no account was George White a jerk himself—he did once try to pay for a shave instead of a haircut after having his head shaved, but that incident was quickly ironed out without anyone getting their head punched in (sort of a rarity for disagreements and misunderstandings in the young city), and people decades later remembered him as "peaceful beyond comprehension." As Canton remembered him, "George was intelligent and smart, and always ready to turn an honest penny in any practicable way, and was ambitious withal."

But he does feature prominently in the stories of two early jerks: Richard Harper, the drunk, and John Stone, the killer.

Harper was a young, educated Eastern man who had been drummed out of the army for being a drunk. He drifted his way to Chicago around 1834, where he quickly made a name for himself as a beggar, a trade by which he earned himself, Canton remembered, "a little food and a great deal of whiskey." Lacking the money to pay rent on a place of his own, he would sleep on piles of shavings or prairie hay, and seemed happy enough with his lot in life. When drunk, he would wander around the streets, swearing in both English and Latin ("when half drunk," it was said, "he was vain of his classics.").

Now and then people would try to scare him out of drinking. When he asked a doctor for a dollar for whiskey one cold night, the doctor said that if Harper drank that night, he would probably freeze to death, but that he'd give him the dollar if he (Harper) would agree to let him dissect his body (this was well under what medical schools generally paid for a corpse at the time). The suggestion was meant to scare Harper into reforming, but he agreed to the deal at once, collected the dollar, and proceeded to live through the night.

Finally, someone got fed up with Harper and complained about him, and he was eventually sentenced to be sold into indentured servitude for thirty days to cover the debts he couldn't pay. The ensuing sale would sometimes be referred to as Chicago's first "slave auction."

George White proclaimed the upcoming sale of a vagrant with "unusual gusto as he paraded down Water Street and back." A constable stood upon a box at Water (now Wacker) and Franklin Streets, and gathered a crowd for the big event.

The "auction" does not seem to have been a particularly serious one—it was more likely just an attempt to humiliate Harper into reforming, and the whole affair seems to have been a parody of a slave auction, not a normal one. The constable spoke of what a fine specimen Harper was, noting his education, his intelligence, his powerful physique, and, especially, "the handy knack he had of putting whiskey where it could not allure the young from the paths of sobriety."

The sole bid for Harper the Drunk came from George White, who bid a quarter and said, "I will take the man for better or worse and without warranty." The sale was approved and White, with what witnesses called "characteristic pomposity," ordered Harper to follow him home.

But Harper ran away and no one seems to have tried to stop him. Some later accounts said that White led Harper away on a rusty chain, and when Harper never did any work, White made a "hundred dollar ruckus" over losing his quarter, ringing his bell and bemoaning his loss every hour on the hour. More likely, though, if White made any such show at all, it was all just in jest.

At the time, it was hoped that the "degrading transaction had stung him so deeply that it would produce a permanent reformation," but Harper's drinking continued on, perhaps even worse than ever, until he left Chicago.

Today, we would recognize that Harper had a disease—people didn't understand alcoholism as well back then. His own jerkiness couldn't be cured simply by humiliating him, and there's an extent to which he couldn't be blamed, as he was powerless over the lure of whiskey. A far bigger jerk, and one who couldn't fall back on such excuses, was John Stone, who would be the first man hanged in Chicago.

By 1840, Chicago was a town of some seven thousand people—a very good size for a town on the old frontier. But most of town was concentrated around the Loop area—anything west of

Halsted was still "the country," and big game still roamed nearby. Once a year, all of the local businesses would close so the men could participate in an annual event in which all the wolves in the woods were chased out onto the icy lake to be killed.

Eight miles out of the city proper, around where the neighborhood known as Jefferson Park is today, there was an establishment owned by one Mr. Rogers known as "Big Woods." Rogers had employed a band of men to cut down the trees in the area to be converted into logs to sell to Chicago, where most of the major buildings were still glorified log cabins. In a shanty nearby, a woman named Lucretia Thompson was employed doing odd jobs, including milking the three or four cows that were given the run of the place.

One day, the men were returning from work and saw that all of the hogs had crowded around one point. In the middle of the hogs they found the murdered, and partially devoured, body of Ms. Thompson. One worker, John Stone, had been heard threatening her recently, so suspicion immediately fell on him. He was arrested and taken to the jail at Randolph and LaSalle, which was, at the time, nothing but a log cabin itself—Stone may have chopped down some of the logs that held him prisoner.

During the trial, it came out that on the day after the murder, Stone had burned his pants, saying that they were "too dirty to wear," an explanation that most found laughable. When asked why he hadn't burned his shirt as well, he quickly replied, "because there was no blood on it."

Stone wasn't just a jerk—he was also apparently a bit of a dumbass.

The jury, which included "Long John Wentworth," who would eventually become the mayor, deliberated for two nights. It was said to be Wentworth who was holding the jury up, and the eager townspeople actually spoke of hanging Wentworth in effigy. But eventually, the jurors all agreed on a verdict of guilty, and Stone was sentenced to hang.

In prison, Stone seemed to accept the verdict. People who came in to find out whether Stone was religious or not found him sitting around, "not appearing unusually dejected." He continued to say that he hadn't murdered Lucretia Thompson, but casually added that he had committed other murders before, so he probably deserved the punishment anyway.

On June 10, the jury and sixty militiamen accompanied Stone on horseback to the place of execution, along with half of the rest of the town (who had come to watch the show). In those days, executions were still a public affair, as public executions wouldn't be outlawed in Illinois for close to a decade, and there existed a class of people that believed them to be first-class entertainment, as well as a good way to teach children a lesson about behaving. The place of execution was down on the South Side dunes—near what is now the intersection of 24th and Indiana.

The rope for the noose was cut and prepared by George White, who would be remembered by a witness to the hanging as "an old colored man who was known around town as a jack of all trades." A simple scaffold and trap door were set up, with a farm wagon beneath it to catch the body when it was cut down.

Stone was taken to the makeshift gallows dressed in a long white gown, and made a little speech (as was the custom at the time). He thanked the sheriff for his kindness (a standard feature of such speeches), and went on to say that he was not only innocent, but he knew two of the people who were really involved in the murder. He declined to name them, though. "I will swing (on the gallows) before I have their blood upon me," he said.

A church service was performed, a hood was lowered over Stone's face, and he was hanged, strangling slowly to death over the course of several minutes. The body was then cut down and given over to doctors for dissection.

White was still listed in the 1843 Chicago city directory as "White, Black George—city crier," but he seems to have died a short while after. No one seems to know for sure what happened to him; the best guess is that he died in the 1840s, was buried in an unmarked grave in the city cemetery, and was likely left behind when the graveyard was moved.

CHAPTER 3

Martin Quinlan
Bribes Weren't All He Took . . .

Chicago has been known for corruption since before it was even a proper city. Rumors of corruption within Fort Dearborn were rampant, and the murder of Jean LaLime may have been covered up so that the corruption could continue on. There is even a story that when Chicago voted to officially incorporate, only 140 people showed up for the ballot and 150 votes were needed, so ten people voted twice, launching Chicago as a city where men would vote early and often.

When the city was young, the corruption went all the way to the bottom rung of the city government. There may be positions lower down the ladder than City Sexton (cemetery manager), but it's hard to imagine what they might be. It was by no means a position they trusted only to the best and brightest.

You wouldn't think such a position, in which most of the citizens under your jurisdiction were corpses, would open one up to too many kickbacks, but Martin Quinlan, a city sexton in the 1850s, found a way to make the job pay off.

The growth of Chicago happened to come about at a time when cemeteries were changing around the world—most rural places had no cemetery at all; the dead were usually just buried on their property. Urban dead were usually put in churchyards, and those got overcrowded quickly. Ancient country churches in England and older American towns today tend to look as though they're sinking into the ground, though they're not, really—the ground has just risen around them as a result of people having been buried nearby them for centuries. And those are just the country churches; the city churchyards were generally smaller spaces where coffins would be buried right on top of other coffins. There were lots of stories about sextons having to jump up and down on top of them to keep them below the surface, hoping that the coffin on the bottom of the stack had decayed enough to collapse and sink down a bit. Seeing bones lying around above the surface was not uncommon.

It should surprise no one that the stench in these places was hideous. It was even said to be dangerous to breathe graveyard air at all, and only truly sick people—and the sexton—ever attended burial services.

In the 1830s, Chicago was right on the cutting edge when it decided to have a "garden cemetery," following the new trend of designating wide-open spaces out in the outskirts of the city where the dead could have some room to breathe, and where families could enjoy a day strolling among the tombs of the departed.

The first official burial grounds in the city had been designated in two spots near the lakeshore—one at about Chicago Avenue (on what was then the "far north" side) and one around 26th Street (the far south). Both were founded at a time when people never imagined that the city would grow much beyond the "loop" area bounded by the north and south branches of the Chicago River. Of course, the city caught up to these grounds quickly, so a large space was eventually designated a mile or two north of the Chicago Avenue cemetery in a pleasant space near the lake, and bodies from the first cemeteries were moved there.

But the growth of these modern cemeteries also came at the same time as the growth of medical colleges. Medicine was finally becoming more of a science than a set of superstitions, and medical schools had figured out that there was no real way to train new doctors without having dead bodies from which to learn the finer points of anatomy—and on which they could practice surgery. But no one donated their body to science in those days, and though many cities granted the bodies of executed convicts to the medical schools, those didn't come in very often—Chicago was known to go years between executions. In its first quarter-century, only a few men were executed.

To respond to the shortage, schools began to have something of an "open-door" policy—anyone who somehow came into possession of a corpse could take it to the medical school to trade in for cash, and no questions would be asked. Most of the schools paid a lot more for a body than mining companies paid for a day of digging for coal; indeed, some paid the equivalent of a month's coal mining salary for a fresh body.

But becoming a grave robber isn't as simple as just taking a shovel and a sack down to the local graveyard and having at it. You have to make sure you won't be caught, which may have required hiring a lookout, and you have to know where the freshest bodies have been laid to rest. It's also wise to have a source who can assure you that the body you're digging up didn't die of smallpox, cholera, or something else you could still catch.

So, in the 1850s, the local grave robbers made friends with Martin Quinlan, the city sexton, who was happy to help.

Not much is known about Quinlan, except that the newspaper once described him as a "border ruffian," a term that historically refers to pro-slavery activists from Missouri who went into Kansas to try to establish it as a slave state (often by force) when it was admitted to the union and allowed to make up its own mind about whether or not to allow slavery. Picking up on the story from afar, the *New York Times* described Quinlan as "a Catholic Irish democratic office holder." He was probably a drifter trying to make his way through the wilderness, like so many who came to Chicago in those days; it was a city famous as a resort for tough vagabond men. How in the world he talked his way into a getting even a low-level government job is anyone's guess, but this was an age when the humblest of jerks could talk their way up the ladder without bothering to be qualified.

We do, however, know that, for a small "honorarium" Quinlan would tell the grave robbers where the best scores would be, and help them make their getaway without being detected. Protection from vigilantes is essential for grave robbers.

Most of the time, Quinlan would point robbers toward bodies buried in the potter's field—the poor section. These graves were generally unmarked, and, being the graves of the poor and friendless, the odds that anyone would notice, or care, that the bodies were missing was low. (Eventually, the city would begin giving all "potter's" bodies to the medical schools outright—a practice they re-initiated in 2011—in an attempt to stop the grave robbers. It wasn't successful; grave robbers could still make a living by digging up Chicago bodies to ship to schools in Ann Arbor.)

But Quinlan made one mistake—he forgot to get the grave digger, the one employee he had to supervise, in on the scheme. In 1856, when "Joe the Gravedigger" noticed that a couple of recent graves from the potter's field had been disturbed, he did some investigating and found that the coffins had been dug up, broken into, emptied out, and reburied. He alerted the Pinkerton Detective Agency, which set up a couple of detectives at the entrance of the graveyard for a stakeout that the *Tribune* described in the most dramatic terms possible:

"It was a solemn watch . . . among the graves of so many dead, and stout hearts that had beat calmly in times of visible peril would have quailed in these silent hours as visions of ghosts and yawning graves came up . . . but the detectives watched on and whatever superstition may have chilled their hearts, they remembered that darkness is ever the favorite cloak of evil and they were impelled to greater vigilance."

This "greater vigilance" paid off—a little before midnight, they saw a wagon being driven into the graveyard and crawled on their hands and knees through the fetid ground. They watched the robbers dig up the bodies, then ran behind the wagon as it left. They caught up with it when it stopped at Chicago Avenue and pounced on the driver, pinning him to the ground by his throat.

The driver was none other than Martin Quinlan.

Quinlan got out from under the detective and tried to make an escape while the detectives chased after the other men who had been in the buggy, but a couple of warning shots stopped him in his tracks. The wagon turned out to contain two bodies—one of a woman, and one of a man who had died after having his legs amputated.

The tomb of Ira Couch is still standing in Lincoln Park, just across the road from the old potter's field.
PHOTO BY AUTHOR

That grave robbing had been a problem in the city was well known—a couple of years before, eleven recent graves had been checked, and only one still contained a body. But this didn't make it okay; Quinlan was fired on the spot. In an editorial following the scandal, the medical school that was paying for the bodies pointed out that if the doctor who had amputated the legs had had more bodies on which to practice, the man probably wouldn't have died in the first place.

Quinlan pleaded guilty to two counts of body snatching and was fined $250 for each offense (about a year's salary for most men at the time). Quinlan's lawyer paid the fine at once, and Quinlan, free to go, left the courthouse with his friends.

The guy who took his job in the 1860s may have been at least as big of a jerk—possibly more of one, depending on your point of view. In their later years, many medical students published memoirs of going to graveyards to snatch the bodies, and one wrote of having bribed the sexton at City Cemetery to tip him off when a group of bodies from Camp Douglas, the South Side Confederate prison, were being delivered to the City Cemetery.

Having gotten the tip that half a dozen bodies were to be left in the "Dead House," the morgue on the south end of the graveyard, and that the dead house would be left unlocked so that he could get in, the student arrived ready to make his score and found the Dead House full of cops, all with pistols drawn, who were waiting to arrest him. The sexton had taken the bribe for the tip and the promise of protection, then informed the police at once (probably for another bribe).

No one knows for sure whatever happened to Martin Quinlan, the border ruffian sexton. Many border ruffians became guerilla soldiers for the Confederacy in the North during the Civil War, and Chicago certainly had its share of "Copperheads" (Northerners who sided with the Confederacy), but Quinlan doesn't seem to have been among them—in 1862, when the war was picking up steam, he was arrested and sentenced to a year in prison in Joliet for the attempted burglary of a cow.

CHAPTER 4

Cap Hyman and George Trussell
Trading Bullets on Randolph

It is currently illegal to have livestock in the Loop.

But as recently as the 1920s, one would still occasionally see a cow wandering down Michigan Avenue, and even now there's a cow path on Monroe Street, just west of Clark. The original owner of the plot of land supposedly put a clause in the contract stating that when he sold it, he had to be allowed to continue using the cow path to lead his cows to a pasture where the Board of Exchange now stands. Years later, when a building was erected on the spot, the construction company somehow convinced the owners that due to the ancient contract, they had to leave room in the building for a cow path. One can imagine that they might have had a good laugh when the owners went along with it; but it's still there. The narrow strip looks like a regular alley today—albeit an alley that cuts right through the middle of a building.

It stands as a reminder of an era when Chicago was, in many ways, a Wild West town. There may not have been many cowboys or shoot-outs on Main Street at high noon, but there were plenty of outlaws. Two particular jerks, George Trussell and Samuel "Captain" Hyman, wandered the saloons and gambling dens of Hairtrigger Block throughout the 1860s, shooting at one another and generally acting like stock characters from a B-movie western.

In the middle of the nineteenth century, Chicago grew faster than any city could manage. Buildings were rising up faster than inspectors could inspect them, and aspiring criminals moved to the booming city in far greater numbers than aspiring police officers. Reformers occasionally swept through the city to tear down vice districts, sometimes quite literally—Mayor Long John Wentworth picked a night when everyone in "the Sands" would be busy at a dogfight to lead a group of police across the Clark Street Bridge

Various con games known among gamblers
UNIVERSITY OF ILLINOIS

to tear down the neighborhood, plank by plank. But well into the twentieth century, finding a brothel or gambling parlor was no real trick in Chicago. The city abounded with vice districts—just going south down State Street in the Loop, one would roll through Whiskey Row and Satan's Mile before coming to the Levee District below 12th (Roosevelt) Street—and taking a right turn at any point could land you in some place that was even worse, like Hell's Half Acre, which was estimated to house about four dozen whiskey bars, a few dozen brothels, and at least one opium den, or Little Cheyenne (in those days, Cheyenne was known as the worst of the railroad towns. In retaliation for giving our worst neighborhood such a name, Cheyenne residents starting calling their own vice district "Little Chicago.").

And if you turned right on Randolph, just around the corner from City Hall, and right across the street from the offices of the *Chicago Times,* you'd find yourself on Hairtrigger Block. One paper said that this section had become "so contaminated by . . . execrable vagabonds that respectable persons avoid them as they would a cesspool."

Some, however, say that Hairtrigger Block wasn't really all that bad—in the 1940s, the *Tribune* said the term merely reflected "the grotesque humor of an earlier period" that became a "civic jest" mainly because of the antics of Cap Hyman and George Trussell, a pair of pillars of the gambling community who bought protection from the police and liked to shoot at one another on Randolph Street.

Indeed, an 1862 map of the business district makes Hairtrigger Block seem like any other street—businesses include a fruit shop, an oyster shop, an engraver, and other such innocuous establishments. But among these are a lot of spaces where the business name has simply been left blank. And one of those, on 81 Randolph, isn't listed on the map at all. It was here that Cap Hyman operated a card house. The same also leaves a blank space at 75 Randolph, where Seneca Wright ran the saloon where George Trussell eventually met his end.

What it was that turned these two men against each other seems to have been lost to history, but the two men were known to hate each other, and, once they'd had a few drinks (as they pretty generally did), they would loudly boast that they would shoot the other on sight.

Operating on the same block, they were known to run into each other often, and they would exchange shots on Randolph Street from time to time. Both of them, however, were notoriously lousy shots, and their shoot-outs never did any more damage than poking holes in the street signs.

Hyman didn't seem like a jerk to most who knew him. In fact, he was a pleasant, jovial man when he was sober. But when he was drunk, or on a losing streak, he was quick to reach for his gun. Little is really known of his personal history—some say he was a "English Jew," others that he was a Virginia Copperhead.

George Trussell, his rival, was a quieter guy—some believed that, as a young man, he had a promising career in front of him as a "useful and honorable member of society," but he fell into the life of a degenerate shortly after he discovered gambling. Little is known of his early life, either, but as a young man he worked as a (presumably) honest bookkeeper in a couple of Chicago shops.

It was supposedly one of his customers who introduced him to the joys of faro, a card game that was among the most popular in the Wild West. It required only a single deck, and not too many more brain cells, but it could accommodate any number of players, and offered slightly better odds of winning than most card games. But good odds or bad, Trussell had soon lost all his money, and most of his good reputation, playing the game. No longer employable in the traditional sense, Trussell felt that he had no choice but to embark on a less honest career and open a "faro bank" of his own.

Like Hyman, he was generally a pleasant, likable guy when he was sober or winning, but he wasn't sober very often. His real downfall, though, was not drinking or gambling, but his ill-fated relationship with a woman named Mollie who ran a "resort" of her own (being romantically involved with the owner of a brothel was an essential status symbol for notable gamblers of the day). George and Mollie had a sort of off-again-on-again affair, and his attempts to rid himself of her tended to bring out the worst in both of them. One day on Randolph Street she surprised him and grabbed him, begging him to take her back. Trussell lost his temper and beat her badly on the street as spectators watched.

She would eventually get her revenge. Mollie had come to Chicago from Columbus, Ohio, where, the *Tribune* wrote, "she had been seduced from the path of virtue." She and Trussell became an item, and may have had a child together (she claimed her son was Trussell's, but no one really knew for sure—the kid was taken away and sent to school in Indiana, where, it was said, he had no idea that his mother was a part of the Chicago underworld). The two were engaged at one point, but never married.

When George died in a Randolph Street saloon in 1866, Mollie was hysterical. "Oh, my God!" she shouted in the police station. "He is dead, he is dead. I know it, for I saw him laid out. Oh, how I wish I were dead with him. I know I cannot live now, but I cannot go to heaven. I know I have been wild, and now I will never have any more peace."

According to the papers, she went on in this vein for a long, long time. But nowhere in the pathetic monologue did she mention the fact that George had died because she herself had shot him three times.

Trussell had been hanging around Seneca Wright's saloon, one of the great haunts of Hairtrigger Block, trying to get one "Mr. Austin of the Circus Company" to sing a drinking song called "Limerick Races." They were still bugging Austin to start singing when Mollie stormed into the door.

By this point, they had been separated for two years, but Mollie had never accepted the breakup. She arrived at the saloon in a beautiful white dress, loudly begging Trussell to go out on the town for the night with her. His attempts to politely refuse were rejected, and he eventually put his hands on her shoulders and tried to push her out the door.

Mollie reacted to this treatment by pulling out a pistol, aiming it, and firing it into George's side. As he clutched his side and fell, she fired another shot into his back at point-blank range. She shot him in the side again as he stumbled out of a side entrance into a stable.

Trussell died instantly, a bullet having pierced his heart. The inconsolable Mollie served only a few months in prison before being pardoned (it's generally assumed that she had a connection or two), and she eventually migrated to California.

Seeing what could happen when you promised marriage but didn't deliver, Cap Hyman promptly married his girlfriend, a madam known as Gentle Annie Stafford—some say she talked him into the marriage with the aid of a horsewhip.

"Hyman was an insufferable egotist," wrote Frederick Francis Cook in 1911, "and his irascible temper was forever getting the whole street in trouble. Again and again, after some ineffectual target practice on his part, the press would read the riot act to the authorities—a proceeding which now and then resulted in a general 'shake-up,' but seldom until the valiant 'Cap' had found it convenient to absent himself for a month or two on important business."

Having gotten married, Cap attempted to go straight, opening a high-end resort on the North Side with Stafford, where they made a show of discussing poetry with the upper crust. Annie's opening line for conversations was "Who's your favorite poet? Mine's Byron," which sounded a bit odd when she asked it while pointing a pistol at people, as she occasionally did when people resisted her attempts at genteel conversation. Indeed, once the reporters had left on opening night, the place immediately declined into the scene of a drunken fight. Cap shot out the lights while Annie wandered around the ruckus, still trying to get discussions about poetry started.

Though he tried to live a respectable life, Cap's appetite for gambling and brothels was unabated. In 1868, in fact, he did perhaps the jerkiest thing a person can do in a bar fight, short of actually killing someone: He shot a guy in the groin.

Exactly what was going on at the New York Sample Room, a saloon on South Clark, in full view of the nearby courthouse, on that fateful night in 1868, is hard to tell for sure, but the general story can be figured out just from the few facts that we know. The Sunnyside Resort had closed down and taken all of Hyman's money with it, and he was presumably in one of his trademark bad tempers. He entered the saloon around midnight.

As he and several others drank at the bar, a dispute arose over who was going to be paying the tab. One man, a proprietor of another saloon, said that Hyman still owed him money for drinking at his place, and Hyman responded by firing a revolver at him. It was only a blank in the chamber, and the man's life was spared, but the second shot was a live round, which went into the groin of the son of one of the owners of the New York Sample Room. The shot wasn't fatal, but the victim was carried to his parents' house, where he suffered unbearable agony for a few days as doctors attempted to get the bullet out of his groin.

Like Mollie before him, Cap Hyman's connections allowed him to go free, but his days of living large were over. In an attempt to put resorts and gambling parlors behind him, Cap tried to open a candy store—but choosing his old Randolph Street stomping grounds for a location was probably not a wise move to start with, and he lost everything when it was destroyed in the Great Chicago Fire. A few years later Hyman died penniless and insane in a low-down rooming house.

CHAPTER 5
Wilbur F. Storey
The Cable News Loudmouth of His Day

A significant amount of my time is spent digging through old newspaper and magazine articles. It's always interesting to read these with the benefit of hindsight; from our own vantage point in history, we can easily see which papers were the most politically astute, which ones *really* had a decent idea what was going on in Washington, and which seemed to have any sense at all of how the world was going to grow and change.

The papers from the late nineteenth and early twentieth century in Chicago can be particularly entertaining. William Randolph Hearst was a pioneer in tabloid journalism; though his papers can never, ever be considered a reliable source for information, they're still remarkably entertaining to read. Hearst's papers never let facts get in the way of a good story and were not above fudging the facts to push the United States into war. When a scandal broke, they could usually be counted on to print the wildest rumors of any paper in town.

But of all the old papers from Chicago, the most shocking to read today is the old *Chicago Times,* which was published by Wilbur F. Storey, the most vocal critic of Abraham Lincoln the city ever produced. So incendiary was his paper that Union general Ambrose Burnside actually tried to shut it down—only intervention from Lincoln himself allowed the paper to keep running.

Today, Ambrose Burnside is remembered more for his resplendent facial hair than anything else, and this is probably the best

Wilbur F. Storey, trying to look respectable
CHICAGO HISTORY MUSEUM

way to honor his memory; looking at his hapless career in the military isn't going to do his legacy any favors.

But Wilbur F. Storey is barely remembered at all. When his name is mentioned, it's usually just when someone quotes his savage review of Lincoln's Gettysburg Address, which has become sort of famous in Civil War circles and is often quoted by writers wanting to show that the initial reaction to the speech was not uniformly positive. They seldom mention, though, that Storey was a complete crank.

Storey came to Chicago and bought the *Times* in 1861 with the intention of continuing its original purpose—the paper had been an organ to support "Douglas Democracy," pushing the policies of Senator Stephen Douglas, who had just been defeated in his bid for the presidency by Abraham Lincoln in the 1860 election. Lincoln had made a name for himself in a series of debates against Douglas, who was a bit of a jerk himself. Any time you see a quote where Lincoln said something that sounds horribly racist by today's standards, it's a safe bet that he said it because Douglas talked him into a corner during one of those debates.

Though Douglas had plenty of accomplishments to be proud of under his belt (like getting the railroad to Chicago), his legacy is rather tainted by his position on race and slavery. It was he who proposed the Nebraska Kansas act, which ended the Missouri Compromise (the rule that slavery would not exist in states farther north than Missouri) and made every new state added to the union a battleground for slavery. Though he may have privately opposed slavery in principle, he wasn't above using the racism of the times to his own advantage, and he tried to buddy up to slave-holding states with an eye toward gaining their support in his presidential bids.[1]

But the paper's influence had dwindled down to nothing over the years and probably didn't seem to have a bright future when the recently defeated Senator Douglas died—and the Civil War began—just around the time that Storey took over. Without Douglas's agenda to push, Storey was left to transform it into the most vocal "Copperhead" (anti-Union) paper.

---

1 Today, one can walk right into the tomb at the base of his monument on the Near South Side. There are brochures about his life set up right on his sarcophagus. This is kind of tacky, in a way, but he was sort of a jerk, so . . .

*There are no known photos of Storey's "castle,"
but some newspaper illustrations survive.*
CHICAGO TRIBUNE

While the Chicago press had generally been dominated by fairly upright papers before, Storey brought an element of the sensational to the press. It was he who wrote what may be the most notorious headline in Chicago newspaper history—reporting on a hanging, the simple headline read "Jerked to Jesus." The hanging in question wasn't even in Chicago—Storey just liked to write about hangings.

Under Storey, though, the paper became profitable for the first time in its history, and soon they'd moved into a fine new office on Randolph Street, just across the street from Hairtrigger Block, where the staff would occasionally hear the sounds of George Trussell and Cap Hyman shooting at one another.

Storey's motto was to "print the news and raise hell," and the paper lived up to it. *Times* reporters used to say that his editorials were so incendiary that you could see blue smoke rising from the ink. Today, the image that comes to mind when one reads his editorials is more of a man frothing at the mouth—he would have done great on cable news.

While it's common to hear now that the Civil War had little or nothing to do with slavery, few people seemed to think this during the war itself. Storey, for one, was certain that Lincoln was using the war to push for racial equality and an end to slavery, and this was a large part of why he opposed the war. Most papers of the day occasionally dipped into racism; Storey's practically rejoiced in it.

Typical of his editorials is the one he wrote in April 1863, after the first group of black recruits for the Union Army left the city to go and fight:

> *[The legion] was headed by the sooty officer, immediately behind whom was a drummer, whose professional acquirements in this line were confined to the ability to keep wretched time. A shade with a tin horn was upon his left, while the cheek of a grinning gorilla was laid lovingly upon a violin upon his right . . . at a given signal, the drum was struck . . . the sable Captain shouted "Fow wad march," and the whole party moved off, singing "Darkeys, de day ob freedom am dawnin". . . . they swaggered and rolled from side to side like a duck attempting locomotion on dry land, and formed a column which, in its vibrations, somewhat resembled the letter S. The men were some of them humpbacked, some round-shouldered, others knock-kneed or pigeon-toed. . . . the odor emitted from that vast throng of shades was truly appalling.*
>
> *At last the cars moved off, greeted with cheers by the crowd and the waving of handkerchiefs, which was responded to by a song, "When We Get Back, We'll Have Uncle Abe's Daughter," which was born back upon the wind as the train moved away in the distance, for, as it dashed down past the avenue, the "sojers" kept yelling and shrieking like a cargo of fiends.*

He further made a point of quoting one of the recruits as referring to the publisher of his rival paper, the *Chicago Tribune,* as "the nigger's friend."

It was his reaction to the Gettysburg Address, though, that would make Storey the answer to Civil War trivia questions for years to come. Lincoln's famous speech was only a couple of minutes long, and came after a windy two-hour speech by Edward Everette. It was met with silence—whether it was an awed or disappointed silence is a matter of some debate.

Though the press around the country generally liked the speech much more than the crowd seemed to, Storey was appalled. "The cheek of every American must tingle with shame," he wrote, "as he reads the silly, flat, and dishwatery utterances of the man who has to be pointed out to intelligent foreigners as the President of the United States." He went on to claim that Lincoln was now using the war as a vehicle to fight slavery.

On this point, though, Storey was actually being fairly astute (for once). Though most critics praised the speech, only a few truly noted that with the address, Lincoln had redefined the purpose of the war, making the end of slavery one of its official goals (the official purpose, before, had merely been to preserve the Union, though when it became clear that this would be a real war, not just a dust-up, people came to realize that if slavery wasn't ended by it, they'd just end up fighting it all over again sooner or later).

Storey took particular issue with the notion put forth in the speech that "our forefathers" had conceived of a nation "dedicated to the proposition that all men are created equal." This, he said, was a perversion of history. He went on to quote the section of the Constitution that stated that all men were not created equal—slaves were only counted as three-fifths of a person in the Constitution.

"It was to uphold this constitution," Storey seethed, "that our officers and soldiers gave their lives at Gettysburg. How dared he, then, standing on their graves, mis-state the cause for which they died, and libel the statesmen who founded the government? They were men possessing too much self-respect to declare that negroes were their equals, or were entitled to equal privileges."

But this was a perversion of history on Storey's own part, too—Lincoln was talking about the men from "four score and seven years ago" who signed the Declaration of Independence in 1776, which *did* state that all men were created equal. Storey was quoting the Constitution, which was written more than a decade later by a somewhat different group of forefathers.

When there wasn't anything interesting coming over the telegraph to be reported on in the papers, Storey simply made stuff up. "When there's no news," he told one reporter, "just print rumors." As the war progressed, Storey began to dip into wild conspiracy theories that would look right at home on even the wildest political message boards today—his editorials don't resemble modern newspaper articles so much as modern YouTube comments. He began to allege that Lincoln was using seances to get war advice from the late Senator Douglas (perhaps thinking that if things went well with the war, the paper could *still* find a way to credit Douglas instead of giving Lincoln even passing praise). Lincoln did attend a seance or two, like practically everyone else in those days, but he seems to have thought of them as nothing more than first-class entertainment, not as a serious way to communicate with the dead.

General Burnside was so appalled by the paper that in 1863, he sent Storey the following telegram:

> *EDITOR OF THE CHICAGO TIMES:*
> *You are hereby notified that I have issued an order stopping the publication of your paper. . . . You will please govern yourself accordingly.*

The ban lasted only a couple of days before Lincoln himself ordered the paper to be re-opened. Storey, clearly very pleased with himself, milked the story for weeks. He even wrote and published a long parody of the popular Union song "The Battle Cry of Freedom," the last verse of which ran:

> For the rights of the white man, hurrah, boys, hurrah
> where God put the negro, there let him be
> rally but for the white man and maintain the law
> shouting the battle-cry of freedom

This was the only official battle with the military Storey ever fought, though plenty of stories went around that soldiers passing through were planning to "sack old Storey's Copperhead *Times*" when they were in town. None ever carried out the threat, but Storey was ready if they did—the office was stocked with rifles and grenades, and the boilers were built in such a way that the first floors could be easily filled with scalding steam to repel attacks.

During Lincoln's re-election bid in 1864, Storey railed that Lincoln was cheating. One headline screamed "Plots of Old Abe to Carry the Election in Illinois: No One Except 'Loyal Men' to be Allowed to Vote."

The Democratic Party held its convention in the South Loop that year to nominate General George McClellan, who had previously been in command of the Union Army, and whose combat strategy seems to have been to sit on his butt for two years making Lincoln look bad in order to make him an easy target in the election. The *Tribune* described the convention as an amateurish affair held in a tent. Storey described it as something akin to the Second Coming, with McClellan's nomination sending waves of joy and relief throughout the city.

Over and over again, Storey portrayed himself as the only man in the city who truly understood what was happening in the world, and as the only voice of reason. As the war began to wind down, and it became obvious that the Union would win (which Storey had denied was possible), he had to tone down his criticism and insistence that the war was a waste of time and money, though he grumpily claimed that it would have been won far sooner if someone else had been president.

When Lincoln was assassinated, Storey treated the slain president with respect and generally acted as though he'd supported him all along—though he couldn't resist throwing out an editorial pointing out that John Wilkes Booth, Lincoln's assassin, was certainly no worse than John Brown, the wild-eyed abolitionist who had tried to start a slave uprising in the 1850s. They were, he said, simply two sides of the same coin.

After the war, he had less reason to rail and turned his wrath on "indecent" opera houses and dancers (one of whom got revenge by assaulting him in the street with a horsewhip).

But perhaps his most notable legacy in Chicago history comes from the days following The Great Chicago Fire, when he invented the story that the fire had started when Catherine O'Leary, an Irish "old hag" as he called her, had started the fire. He initially said that she had started the fire intentionally to get even with the city for removing her from the pension rolls, and, a week later, relented a bit and said that the fire hadn't been intentional, but that she had stupidly left a kerosene lantern next to the cow, who kicked it over and started the fire.

The tale had no basis in fact, but Storey used the city's widespread anti-Irish sentiment to spread it around until it became a part of Chicago history that every Chicagoan knew. Few who taught the story to school children pointed out that it was first told by a man who, by 1880, was being sued for slander and libel so often that he stopped paying attention to the suits at all.

As the years went by and Storey became older, he lost what little grip on his sanity he had—many now believe that he was suffering from syphilis. By the end, he was claiming to receive guidance from the spirits themselves, the very course of action that he'd criticized Lincoln over. On the advice of a female Indian spirit named "Little Squaw" (who called him "White Chief"), he began construction on a "wigwam" for himself—a grand, ridiculously expensive white marble mansion, which people called "a castle" to his face and "The Storey Folly" behind his back.

His mental faculties had clearly fallen off. Though he had the money to have the house built, the costs spiraled out of control as he (and the voices in his head) called for changes in the middle of construction. He would walk through the unfinished building and shout, "See there! The snakes are coming through the floor! This house is full of snakes!" and order it redone to get rid of the snakes—which were invisible to everyone else (it's possible that he was hearing the sound of the plumbing and thinking it was a hissing snake, or even seeing the exposed pipes and thinking they were snakes). But he could not be reasoned with, and expensive changes were ordered. But even as his sanity was openly questioned, he continued to edit the *Times* right up until his death in 1884. After eight years of sitting empty, his "castle" was torn down in 1892. His rival newspaper men of the day were as polite as they could be about his declining mental health and spoke in their obituaries of his intellect, his passion, and his austerity.

Today, though, no one speaks of any of those qualities when they talk about him. When he's remembered at all, he's just thought of as another racist Copperhead jerk whose work served as a template for countless journalists who learned the lesson that you could take a bankrupt paper and make it hugely successful just by foaming at the mouth, and his legacy is visible on every cable and radio news channel every day.

The "Storey Castle" survives only in a couple of drawings, though the marble was supposedly used in many of the buildings that still stand nearby in Bronzeville today. One shudders (or perhaps chuckles) to think how he would react to find out that the site he chose for it was only blocks away from the future home of a black man who would be elected president.

CHAPTER 6

Thomas Hines
Architect of Conspiracy

Not all of the jerks in Chicago history were actually Chicagoans at all. Some of them were just guys who came here to do something jerky to the city, like Thomas Hines, the Confederate spy behind a plot to liberate Camp Douglas, the Confederate prison on the Near South Side, and take over Chicago on Election Day, 1864. Like most failed Confederate plots and campaigns, it probably wouldn't have really cost the Union the war if it had succeeded, but it would have thrown the Midwest into chaos for a while and may have drawn the war out a bit longer.

Of course, had *that* happened, it's tempting to imagine that history would have changed just enough that Lincoln wouldn't have gone to Ford's Theatre on the night he was killed, and that he could have survived to serve his second term. Few topics in American history inspire more "what if" than the Civil War.

Like most things to do with the Civil War, historians don't agree today on what really went on with the "Northwest Conspiracy," as it came to be known. Some historians claim that the whole thing was a hoax perpetrated by Colonel B. J. Sweet, commandant of the Chicago troops, in order to make himself look like a hero who had thwarted the Confederates' evil plan. Others say that the Confederates had dreamed up the plot, but never could have possibly carried it out, and that Sweet just pretended they could have.

This sort of thing happens now and then—it calls to mind the time a few years after 9/11 when the Department of Homeland Security announced that they had caught a bunch of guys who were planning to blow up the Sears Tower. And they were planning to blow it up, but as interviews with them and details of their organization came to light, it quickly became apparent that this was a band of slobs who couldn't have blown up a potato in the

Thomas Hines wasn't great as a spy, but he was a master at escaping after his plans failed.
LIBRARY OF CONGRESS

microwave, let alone a skyscraper, on the best day of their lives. There were, in fact, plans to liberate Camp Douglas and seize Chicago, but in practice it was little more than pie-in-the-sky dreaming by a group that probably couldn't have liberated a herd of cattle from an unguarded pen.

But most of the newspapers of the day always treated the Northwest Conspiracy as though it were a real plot—and occasionally as though it had been an actual threat. The fact that it may have been impossible to carry out doesn't mean that Hines was less of a jerk for planning it.

Camp Douglas, sometimes known as "Eighty Acres of Hell," was one of the most notorious of all Northern Civil War prisons. One of the earliest prisoners was Dr. Henry Morton Stanley, who would later make a name for himself searching for David Livingstone in Africa (he's the guy who said, "Dr. Livingstone, I presume"). Of his arrival at Camp Douglas, he wrote that "our buildings were swarming with vermin; the dust sweepings were alive with them. The men began to suffer from bilious disorders; dysentery and typhus began to rage. Day after day my company steadily diminished, and every morning I had to see them carried in their blankets to the hospital whence none ever returned . . . exhumed corpses could not have present[ed] anything more hideous than dozens of these . . . men, who, oblivious to the weather, hung over the latrines or lay extended along an open sewer, with only a few gasps intervening between them and death. Such as were not too far gone prayed for death."

More than a third of the fifteen thousand-odd prisoners held at the prison over the course of the war died there, and stories of the cruelties of the officers are the stuff of legend—surely there will be many who think that Colonel B. J. Sweet, who was in charge in 1864, should be the real subject of this chapter, not Hines. Sweet's daughters would roam the grounds, singing, "Are you all dead yet?" to the tune of the sick call that the bugler played.

But this was war, after all, and Stanley also said, "I admit that we were better fed than the Union prisoners. It was the age that was brutally senseless and heedlessly cruel. It was lavish and wasteful of life."[2]

These miserable prisoners were the men that Thomas Hines hoped would be able to lay waste to Chicago if he only got them out of jail.

Not yet thirty when the war began, Thomas Hines looked a lot like John Wilkes Booth[3] with his curly hair and bushy mustache (in fact, he would eventually get in some hot water after being mistaken for him while Booth was on the run after assassinating Lincoln). He joined the Confederate Army in the autumn of 1861 and quickly rose through the ranks, despite his initial disinterest in fighting anywhere except for Kentucky. Defending his home state was all he cared about; indeed, it was all a lot of soldiers cared about. Those who say the South seceded for reasons other than slavery are kidding themselves, but it's true that many, if not most, soldiers simply felt that they were defending their homes, not fighting for any given political interest.

After Brigadier General John Hunt Morgan made him a captain, Hines spent most of the war dressed in plainclothes and operating alone on a variety of secret missions (in between trips home to visit his family and girlfriend). He was captured and escaped on multiple occasions, and his activities were so secretive that some of his superiors didn't even know he was a spy at all; one described him as "apparently the most listless and inoffensive youth that was ever imposed upon."

But Hines led a party of a couple dozen soldiers on an exploratory mission into Indiana in 1863 to lay groundwork for Morgan's Raid into the Indiana and Ohio regions. After being captured, he wound up in prison near Columbus, Ohio, from which he escaped

---

2 Stanley got out of the camp in six weeks by switching sides and enlisting in the Union Army.

3 Booth had a bit of a history in Chicago as well—in the earliest days of the war, he did a couple of stints playing notable Shakespeare roles at McVicker's Theatre on Madison Street. The *Tribune* called him a genius. One can only imagine how odd it must have been for those who saw him to remember his speeches as Hamlet, Richard III, and Macbeth plotting to kill kings! While in town he stayed at the Tremont House, where Lincoln had made speeches from the balcony.

by tunneling his way out. As he made his way back to Richmond, the capital of the Confederacy, he twice evaded Union soldiers who had sentenced him to death by hanging.

Once in Richmond, he met with Confederate President Jefferson Davis and talked him into backing a plan to free Confederate prisoners who were being held in Union cities, allowing them to burn the cities and cause a mass panic. Davis and his cabinet agreed, though they were a bit concerned about how it would make the Confederacy look to Great Britain and France (for whose support the Confederacy was fairly desperate, though they probably never would have gotten it without outlawing slavery first).

Hines and a band of men traveled to Toronto, then a hotbed of Copperhead activity, and came to Chicago just in time for the Democratic Party National Convention that nominated former Union General George McClellan to run against Abraham Lincoln. Tens of thousands of Copperheads had gathered in Chicago for the event, which was held near 12th Street (now Roosevelt) and Michigan Avenue, just a brisk walk away from Camp Douglas, the former Union training camp that was now being used as a Confederate prison. Upon arriving, Hines met up with the leading members of a secret Copperhead organization known as the Knights of the Golden Circle to make plans.

The prison camp was to be attacked by four parties, with a fifth party waiting a few hundred yards away to supply the freed prisoners with guns. The various parties would surround the camp, break down the walls, and attack the rest of the Union garrison to force them to surrender. When the prison was in their hands, small bands would be dispatched to cut telegraph wires and gain control of the train stations, then the whole group would gather at the court house, effectively putting Chicago into rebel hands.

But word of the conspiracy had already leaked, and Hines was followed into Chicago by Union counterspies. A double agent in his confidence was passing information back to Colonel B. J. Sweet, who eventually led a sweep on the would-be conspirators the day before Election Day, when the plan was to go into action.

Prisoners at Camp Douglas
LIBRARY OF CONGRESS

After the news broke, the city was frightened enough by the supposed raid that federal soldiers protected Chicagoans on their way to the polls the next day, as they turned out to help re-elect Lincoln (who defeated McClellan in a landslide). For weeks, citizens bolted their doors at night.

Maurice Langhorne, a Confederate soldier and veteran of the plot, felt that they came very close to succeeding in liberating the prison and taking the city. Remembering the plot in 1898, he said that he and several other Copperheads arrived in Chicago during the Democratic convention. They felt good about their chances as they gathered in the Richmond Hotel at Michigan and Lake in a room with a sign bearing the words MISSOURI DELEGATION on the door.

"We estimated our strength in Chicago at about 2,000 men and officers in various hotels, boarding and lodging houses," he wrote. "These men were liberally supplied with money." But it was announced that the raid would not take place once the convention nominated McClellan, whose election, they felt, was assured. Defeating Lincoln in the election would be just as great of a boon for the Confederacy. There was no need to carry out the raid that summer after all.

But the infrastructure for the plot was still in place. Confederates had been stationed with flammable materials in many houses. The plan was to set fire to the hotel rooms at one o'clock in the morning, then leave with the keys, attracting the attention of most of the city's firefighters. They had gathered the home addresses of every bank officer, and plans were made to capture them and loot the banks. All of the data and men they needed were still in place should the election look likely to tip to Lincoln, after all.

With the conspiracy abandoned for the moment, Langhorne went to Canada, where he deserted the Confederate Army and began selling information (some of which he likely made up) to the US government.

He returned to Chicago on Halloween intending not to raid it but to settle there and practice law. By chance, he ran into one of his former co-conspirators, who told him that circumstances had changed. Since the convention, General Sherman had captured Atlanta and was now engaged on a march through Georgia. His progress was making it seem as though the war could be winding down, and Lincoln's chances of re-election had improved dramatically. The raid Hines had planned was back on. A hardware store would be arming hundreds of Confederates, he said, so that Camp Douglas could be raided, and every stable could be robbed. Hines was returning to the city on November 5, just in time to burn the city down on the eve of the general election.

Langhorne (if his story is to be believed) quickly reported this to Colonel Sweet, who had his soldiers arrest anyone they could possibly say was a conspirator. As the story spread and the city became shocked at how close they'd come to being invaded, Sweet triumphantly told the press that he had saved the Union. Shortly before Christmas, he was presented with a magnificently decorated sword in honor of his achievement.

Hines would later say of Langhorne that "a blacker-hearted villain never lived." But by most modern accounts, the bigger traitor to his plans was John T. Shanks, whom Hines had set up as the man who would lead the attack on the main gate. Shanks, too, was a double agent. On November 7, the night before the election, it was Shanks who led the Union raid on the Richmond Hotel in which supposed conspirators were rounded up.

Eventually, well over a hundred men were arrested. Two of the conspirators were captured in a house only thirty paces from the prison's main entrance—a huge arsenal of double-barrel shotguns and Colt revolvers were found in the house.

Hines himself made one of his characteristic escapes. When Union troops arrested conspirator Vincent Marmaduke at the Adams Street home of Dr. Edward W. Edwards, Hines was hiding inside a mattress. The next day, he hid his face under an umbrella and snuck back out of the city.

It's difficult today to get to the bottom of what *really* happened with Hines and his great "Northwest Conspiracy"—practically all of the information on it comes from stories told by veterans who, almost invariably, spoke of themselves as the hero who had saved the Union at the last minute.

Though the *Tribune* spent years speaking of the conspiracy as a major campaign that only fast thinking from Sweet and his men had thwarted, Democratic-leaning papers immediately said that the whole thing was a hoax put on to galvanize Republicans and boost Lincoln's chances at re-election. Wilbur F. Storey alleged that the "conspiracy" consisted of only six men, four of whom were actually undercover detectives. "Four detectives leading on two fools!" he raged.

And, for once, he may not have been far off. Of 150 men who were arrested, only eight weren't quickly paroled.

So Hines's conspiracy never quite got off the ground, but Hines certainly *had* made plans to take over Chicago. It seems unlikely that he had nearly enough support in the city to pull it off, though; Hines was a lot better at escaping than he was at actually carrying out raids.

But it's also not exactly ridiculous to imagine that given the right amount of help, the prisoners *could* have overwhelmed the guards (whom they outnumbered by a margin of about ten to one) and taken over. Given the notoriously poor conditions at the prison, it's difficult to imagine that the malnourished prisoners would have been in any condition to function in such a raid to begin with, but some men who were there thought it was possible.

For years afterward, the *Tribune* occasionally carried memoirs from various "conspirators" who detailed the plans they had made to make the raid. "Twenty thousand rebels in the heart of the enemy's country would have changed the aspect of things somewhat!" boasted George Ellsworth in 1882. But, alas, he had been forced to escape. "All of 'our air castles' had vanished," he wrote, "and we were compelled to abandon an undertaking that, had it been successful, would have carried a little of the war into Illinois."

Colonel Dulaney, another Confederate veteran of the plan, claimed, "The prisoners were thoroughly organized, and perfectly familiar with our plans. They were organized into regiments, battalions, and companies, and to a man were ready to make the fight or break for liberty whenever the order, or rather the signal, was given." In Dulaney's version of the story, it was John Shanks ratting them out that foiled the plot. "For Shanks's treachery," he sneered, "he received $5,000 and a commission as Captain in the United States army, and some years afterward was killed and scalped by Indians on the frontier." Though still clearly seething with rage at Shanks, Dulaney did say at the time that the result of the war was "the best thing that ever happened to the South."

So, though by election night the notion that they could have actually carried off the raid seems almost ridiculous, there were certainly people in high places who felt that they had a conspiracy going, and there's something about the Civil War that makes historians want to play "what if." Could Hines ever have liberated Camp Douglas? If a few more stars had aligned, and Hines had had a few more lucky breaks, it seems plausible that he really *could* have had a few thousand armed Copperheads organized, which could have been sufficient to overwhelm the guard of eight hundred at the festering prison.

One can easily imagine nine thousand Confederate soldiers, newly armed and thirsty for vengeance after their brutal treatment in prison, streaming through the city, setting it ablaze just as Sherman had burned Atlanta, taking control of government buildings as Confederate ironclad battleships sailed into Lake Michigan. In Hines's grand scheme, it would have been the first step in sparking a "revolution" that put the whole of the Midwest into Confederate hands, and in later years, some even believed that this would have given the Confederacy the recognition by England and France that it so desperately wanted.

And the sheer fact that he had made plans to burn Chicago to the ground, and even took steps toward making it happen, qualifies Thomas Hines as one of Chicago's greatest villains, whether he was a successful one or not.

CHAPTER 7

Marshall Field
Customers First, Employees Last

If you've ever worked a job that involved customer service, such as waiting tables, answering tech-support phone calls, or running a cash register, odds are you wished you could find whatever jerk came up with the phrase "the customer is always right" so you could punch the living daylights out of him.

The actual origin of the phrase is in dispute, but one of the two or three prime suspects for coining it is Marshall Field of Chicago. Even if he didn't coin the exact phrase, he certainly said things *like* it, and was often credited with it during his lifetime.

Good customer service is absolutely essential to business, not to mention being just plain polite. But how many of us have listened to a customer rail that they should still get the sale price on an item, even though the sale ended three months ago? And how often has this customer devolved into shouting personal insults, often ending with something like "no wonder you have to work *here!*" in the midst of making sure we realize that "the customer is always right"?

Years of retail work taught me that angry customers are very *seldom* right. And it may very well be Marshall Field's fault that they think they are.

Not to mention that his word was instrumental in having several men executed for holding a rally in support of the eight-hour workday.

In many ways, Field's is a wonderful "only in America" sort of story. Born in 1834, as a young man he took a job in a dry goods store, and by the middle of the 1860s, he was the owner of a store that bore his name in Chicago. At the time he was in his mid thirties, that store was grossing $125 million a year. In 2010, *Business Insider* listed him among the twenty richest men of all time, with

Marshall Field

a peak fortune, adjusted for inflation, estimated at $66.1 billion in modern money.

In his flagship store on State Street, he pioneered many techniques that are now universal in department stores. He was among the first to have display windows showing off the beautiful goods to passers-by. The perfumes were kept near the entrance, giving the whole place a sweet aroma. There were bargains in the basement. And his employees set a new standard for customer service. He was so successful that he would eventually be known (perhaps not exactly correctly) as Chicago's richest man. By 1900, he was serving 250,000 customers daily and employed eight thousand people. But his policies toward his employees were not nearly as kind as the policies he held toward his customers. Getting a raise didn't happen when you worked for Field—the wage at which he hired you would be the wage at which you worked for life. When a group of messenger boys got together to request a cost-of-living increase, they were fired on the spot. Female employees were expected to dress and act like professionals but weren't paid accordingly— they worked long hours for low pay.

However, we should probably also note that none of this was uncommon at the time, and that Field was quite a philanthropist as well. Though he initially said, "I don't know anything about a museum and I don't wish to know anything about a museum" when approached for a donation to build the grand museum that bears his name, he eventually was convinced that this sort of thing could become his lasting legacy, and The Field Museum is still one of the greatest institutions in Chicago.

But his position on labor will forever taint his legacy.

His own rise to power came about at the same time that organized labor was on the rise, and when riots began to break out in the 1870s, he donated thousands of dollars to build and stock armories around the city to keep striking workers down. With help from his money, the police became far more of a martial force, with regular drills in street fighting. Speakers began referring to the armed guards who would show up to even the most peaceful of labor rallies as "Marshall Field's boys," and papers under Field's influence began to argue that the police's policy on labor riots should be to "shoot to kill."

Naturally, Field wasn't about to allow his own employees to get organized—plenty of people noted that his policy that the customer is always right would be suspended at once if anyone connected to the labor movement entered the store, even as a customer.

The year 1886 was particularly rough for labor in Chicago. The standard workday at the time was ten hours long, and several groups around the city were going on strike to have it lowered to eight. A couple of striking workers were killed that spring, so tensions were running high when a group obtained a permit to hold a rally in Haymarket Square in early May.

The rally wasn't a particularly big deal, really. Though twenty thousand people had been expected, bad weather kept all but two thousand or so away. The police had gone to the nearby Second Regiment Armory Building and armed themselves with guns and billy clubs in case things got out of hand.

Mayor Harrison himself came out on horseback to make sure the meeting was on the level, and he determined that it was. He ordered the police captains to send their men home, then rode off on his horse.

But the police ignored the order.

The permit expired at 10:30 that night. At 10:31, the last speaker was finishing his remarks. The police formed a line and began to march toward the group, guns drawn, as they ordered them to disperse.

The speaker shouted that the gathering was a peaceable one, but he spoke too soon—the police hadn't quite made it to the crowd when the bomb went off in their line.

Someone—no one ever found out who it was for sure—had thrown a hand-held bomb from a nearby vestibule into the line of cops. One of them was killed instantly.

The rest began firing blindly into the crowd.

By the time the dust settled, seven cops were dead, primarily from friendly fire. Also lying dead were plenty of innocent bystanders who had just come to hear the speeches. No one has ever come up with a reliable number for how many casualties there were, but it was probably quite a few—newspapers reported that dozens of bodies littered the ground in the aftermath.

But most of the wounded didn't dare to seek medical care, for fear they'd be arrested simply for having been present at the legally held rally.

For many years, the city's sympathy was on the side of the police officers, and the ralliers were thought of as "reds" or "anarchists." However, as more facts emerged, and as organized labor became more powerful, the general view of the situation changed. The statue of a police officer that once stood on the rally site has been replaced by a statue of men standing on a pushcart, a monument to the workers. All of the men arrested for their connection to the rally had been pardoned by the beginning of the twentieth century—in 1893, Governor Altgeld determined that all eight of the men put to trial were innocent.

But it was too late for five of them.

In the immediate aftermath, though, the ralliers were looked upon as nothing less than the enemies of democracy. Hundreds were jailed, and most of the organized-labor newspapers were shut down (many never restarted). The police announced a great triumph when they arrested Louis Lingg, who police had determined was the man who had thrown the bomb. However, while Lingg was certainly into explosives, later reports indicated that he hadn't attended the Haymarket Rally at all.

Eventually, several men (mostly speakers from the rally) were put on trial. As the story became national news, a few people in the city began to worry that too harsh a punishment would lead to more labor uprising—particularly considering that there was no evidence at all to connect most of them to the bombing. Harsh punishment could create sympathy for the workers.

Several wealthy merchants in the city held meetings at which they planned to push for leniency, but the strong opposition of Marshall Field kept them from becoming too vocal. Marshall Field firmly believed that the men must be punished harshly to send a message to anyone else who would agitate for better working conditions.

Field even managed to have one of his sales clerks put on the jury—no one believed for a second that the man would still have a job if a guilty verdict was not returned. Many believed that Field himself could take the credit when five of the men, including Lingg, were sentenced to hang.

Four of them eventually were executed, but Louis Lingg was not among them. The night before his scheduled execution he bit into a dynamite cap and blew his brains out. But four men, one of whom had started his adult life working for Wilbur F. Storey, were hanged in the old prison in 1886. They went to their doom singing

The Haymarket anarchists are hanged in the old prison.
LIBRARY OF CONGRESS

songs and shouting slogans, though the prison officials declined to let them make speeches on the scaffold. One shouted that "there will come a time when our silence will be more powerful than the voices you strangle today."

And he was right. To many Chicagoans, this is Field's legacy— he was the man who would kill to send a message to anyone who dared to fight for more equitable treatment for workers.

By the time of his death in 1906 at the age of seventy, his wealth was estimated to be close to two hundred million dollars— in 1906 money. In 1905 he was the largest individual taxpayer in the United States, and upon his death he was one of the most respected men in Chicago history.

Except to the organized labor movement.

And to anyone who ever had an obnoxious customer rail that the customer is always right, his most famous phrase, which is cursed by retail employees every day of the year.

CHAPTER 8

Captain George Wellington Streeter
Commander of the Battle of Garbage Hill

Just a few years ago, if you zoomed in closely on the Yahoo! Maps view of downtown Chicago, you would notice some interesting neighborhood designations. For some reason, century-old neighborhood names were still current in the digital map. The downtown and River North area contained neighborhoods such as Towertown, Little Hell, and Swedetown. It was especially odd to look at the Magnificent Mile and the lower Gold Coast area on the map and see it designated as "Shantytown."

And yet, not too many decades ago, that was what the neighborhood was—a stretch of landfill held illegally by a ragtag band of misfits who fought to keep their shacks and shanties with fists, guns, and scalding water in service of their leader, Captain George Wellington Streeter.

There are plenty of con men in Chicago history, but few can rival "Cap" Streeter for sheer audacity. "With little more than bravado, a shotgun, and a presidential forgery," wrote biographer Wayne Klatt, "he claimed responsibility for all 186 acres of the city's Gold Coast, and for years he made a livelihood selling deeds to property he never owned."

Today, when you drive over Lake Shore Drive, just north of Navy Pier, you're actually driving over a landfill. In the days after the Great Chicago Fire, Lake Michigan stretched all the way out to Michigan Avenue (hence the name). In the city's earlier days, when the Loop was essentially the entire city, the farthest street to the East was Dearborn. Everything beyond that was the beach,

The statue of Captain Streeter
PHOTO BY AUTHOR

and the build-up of State Street, Lake Shore Drive, and Michigan Avenue all came from hotel owner Potter Palmer's scheme to build up more luxury retail and residential areas.

But for one stretch of the North Side, we've long given credit to one Captain George Wellington Streeter. According to Streeter's version of the story, his pioneer days began one morning when he was attempting to sail his boat out of the lake, down the river, and into the Gulf of Mexico, where, he said, he planned to work as a gunrunner. But instead of heading south, he ran aground on the lakeshore and, unable to sail away, started charging people money to dump their garbage around his boat. Eventually, he "created" 186 acres of landfill, which he declared to be his own independent state—and, eventually, his own independent country.

The truth is slightly more complicated—it involved a little more bribery, a few more forged deeds, and a rather large handful of lies. He was one of the most colorful figures in Chicago history, but underneath it all, he really was a big jerk. The exact details of what happened when he crashed the boat ashore are buried now under the legalese of a million lawsuits and unreliable documents. At various times the deeds he held to his lands were upheld; at other times they were judged as forgeries.

In truth, the city was already filling in the area—a boulevard (now known as Lake Shore Drive) was being built half a mile out into the lake, and the land was being gradually filled in, largely due to the machinations of Potter Palmer. Through a few dubious legal maneuvers, the city was able to give the ownership of the new land to whomever owned the bit of shoreline it was connected to. The ideas Streeter had—that he had created the land himself, or that he had any claim to it—were just bits of imagination that he was occasionally able to back up in court.

Streeter didn't really even crash ashore—he sailed right up to it. Then, as the land began to be filled in, he simply claimed it as his own. At one point he showed up in court with a list of lawyers who would back up his claim, but none of them had actually signed on; Streeter had just walked around to law offices jotting down names of lawyers. When that wasn't enough to support his claim, he drew up a deed and forged President Cleveland's signature on it, then found an old map showing that the territory of Chicago ended at the old shoreline—everything else was outside of the city's jurisdiction. Confident in his claim, he began to sell lots on the new land.

Soon the "District" was littered with shanties, some of which became what must have been the most ramshackle whiskey bars, brothels, and gambling halls in town.

And the city wasn't about to stand for it. Particular pressure came from the wealthy citizens who had built mansions for themselves along Michigan Avenue; they were not pleased to find that their unobstructed views of the lake had become unobstructed views of a shantytown (which, it bears mentioning, lacked any sanitation facilities).

And so began what some might call the Battle of Garbage Hill, a thirty-year war in which the city and its more respectable citizens fought against Streeter and his band of (mostly) less respectable ones.

The courts went back and forth between ordering Streeter to leave and backing up his claims. Either way, he planned to stay—by force, if necessary. "By all that's living, you can't take me!" he once shouted at men who came to evict him. "Ye're the tools of rich men; slaves and dogs paid to ruin Cap Streeter, but you can't do it!"

And though plenty of the battles of the thirty-year war were fought in court, plenty more fights took the form of actual combat, as Streeter and his ragtag immigrants to the "Deestrict" organized themselves into "Streeter's Army." His wife was known to attack oncoming lawmen with boiling water (and, at least according to legend, the contents of a chamber pot).

Stories of the Captain and his battles with the police and the armed forces became the stuff of legend partly because of the way Streeter succeeded in making them up and spreading them around. Once, the police succeeded in breaking into the houseboat and confiscating most of the Captain's weapons. The angry Streeter went to the police station on his own, unarmed, and somehow managed to hold it hostage for several hours until his guns were returned. Or, anyway, that was the way *he* told the story. One would think that rule No. 1 for dealing with a hostage situation is "never give the hostage taker a big box of guns."

Another time, he successfully defended himself in court against charges of refusing to disperse when he was told to on the grounds that, since he was only one person, he could not possibly "disperse."

Still another time, in 1902, Streeter was actually convicted of murder after one of the battles and was sentenced to life in prison. The governor pardoned him after only nine months, convinced that Streeter's claims of being framed were correct.

While he seemed to base a lot of his own defense on the tried and true methods of lying to the court, forging documents, shooting at people, or throwing poo around, Streeter's argument about land ownership may have had some merit. That the city had any right to create new land in the lake and claim jurisdiction over it was dicey, at best, which was part of why Streeter was able to keep his claim on the land for so long.

But as the city grew, the value of the land he was squatting on grew immensely. Lakefront property was hugely valuable by the time of World War I, and most of "Streeterville" was still sitting vacant, tied down under mountains of red tape.

It wasn't until 1918 that the city finally succeeded in getting rid of the Captain. The courts officially decided that he had no claim on the lands, and he was officially evicted. He never stopped claiming to own the land, but his days of living on it were over.

Streeter had, by this time, become something of a beloved eccentric in the city. Many people hated his guts, but even the ones who couldn't stand him couldn't help but be amused by his antics. A few even called him a hero. Some of these, quite likely, had been swayed by a biography published in 1914. Entitled *Captain Streeter: Pioneer,* it was written by one of his lawyers and portrayed him as a great visionary. It's basically unreadable today.

Some of his admirers were regulars at the Dil Pickle Club, a Near North Side "open forum" where regulars were entertained nightly with plays, music, debates, and speeches by local eccentrics—"anyone who was a nut about something," owner Jack Jones said.

In 1919, only months after he lost his battle, Captain Streeter was an official lecturer for the bohemian crowd at the Pickle. He was scheduled to appear at 8:30 p.m., and arrived fashionably late. Reports of his speech are perhaps the best way of seeing what kind of guy Streeter was when he wasn't out forging grants and shooting birdshot at people who annoyed him.

"I'm glad to see you all, ladies and gen'lemen," he told the crowd. "I haven't made up my mind what I'm goin' to talk about, but . . ."

And from there, he took off into a long tirade in which, it was said, he "discussed everything but the girth control and the ethical code of the antediluvian dinosaurs." In the speech, he went into rants about Riparian rights, liquor, the US Constitution, Germany, class war, George Washington, the police, judges, Ireland, lawyers, Joliet, and freedom (from a modern vantage point, it sounds like a speech from the Libertarian national convention, except for a few digs at the "capitalists" he said controlled the courts).

And, of course, he spoke of "The Thirty Years' War."

The speech was so quotable that the *Tribune* reprinted a few of his bon mots:

—"The constitution says that any president who participates in any foreign wars must be arrested, impeached, an' hung."

—"If pro'bition ain't the dirtiest imposition ever happened upon this country, then I haven't got nothing to say."

—"People oughtn't to be dragged off to prison for arguin'. That's what they done in Ireland, an' what is the result? The Irish is just as bad as ever."

The Captain was apparently quite taken with the Dil Pickle Club. On his deathbed, he willed the presidency of "Streeterville" to Jack Jones, the owner of the club. Jones's own attempts to run people off of the land were awfully short lived—they seem to have lasted less than thirty minutes, as opposed to Streeter's own thirty-year battle. Jones marched onto the beach with a deed in hand signed by "Ma" Streeter, and announced plans to clear others from the land in order to build homes for disabled war vets, chapels for religious "sects," stadiums, and art studios, as well as several low-rent apartment buildings.

Bathers at the beach told them to "beat it." When he didn't, he was arrested, taken away, and released. He and Streeter's heirs kept up the fight, in a half-hearted sort of way, for most of the 1920s, but they were eventually shut down for good.

The Captain died of pneumonia at the age of eighty-four, reportedly with his trademark plug hat on his head. It was placed atop his flag-draped silver casket at his funeral, which was attended by the mayor himself. We still call the neighborhood around the Hancock Building "Streeterville" in his honor.

City authorities may have fought with the Captain, but they were going to miss having guys like him to kick around. It was 1921, after all. Prohibition was in effect, and the city's battles with its citizens were about to get a whole lot more serious.

CHAPTER 9

H. H. Holmes
The Devil of the Murder Castle

When we think of men like H. H. Holmes, we have to use the word *jerk* in its broadest sense. Does being a fiend automatically make you a jerk?

There are subtle differences in various terms for unpleasant people. For instance, *jack off* and *wank* both describe the same physical action, but calling someone a jack-off isn't exactly the same as calling someone a wanker. A jack-off is a big jerk, somewhat more aggressively unpleasant than a wanker, who is really more of a dork, or perhaps a weenie, than a jerk. The Chicago-area variation, *the jag off,* is subtly different still.

So, if a person is generally pleasant to be around, except for the part where he kills you, is he really a *jerk,* per se?

Maybe some Hannibal Lecter types are better phrased as *archfiends* or *villains.* The genteel, charming Holmes, the famous Devil of Chicago, fits both those terms just fine. But he also wiggled out of debts great and small, stole people's wives (while ditching several of his own), and cheated his employees in addition to killing at least a dozen people (and possibly dozens more). Truly, the man was a jerk.

Though volumes have been written on Holmes, we really know fairly little about him. Many of the famous stories that have circulated come from neighborhood gossip that continued after he was long out of the city, and what he said about himself was almost always a lie. One of his most famous quotes ("I was born with the devil in me") came from a newspaper reporter for the *Philadelphia North American* who seems to have made it up, and the confession that he wrote for the *Philadelphia Inquirer* shortly before his execution is notoriously unreliable—he confessed to killing three people who weren't actually dead yet, and a few others who prob-

H. H. Holmes was one of the first famous criminals to have a "mug shot" taken.
LIBRARY OF CONGRESS

ably never existed at all. One woman he confessed to killing, Kate Durkee, marched into her local newspaper office the day after it was published to issue a statement that she had "never been killed, by H. H. Holmes or anyone else." But how many people *did* Holmes kill in his Murder Castle, the hotel he operated on 63rd Street, down the road from the World's Fair that was equipped with everything one could need to kill a person? How many did he kill in his numerous other buildings in Chicago, or on his travels around North America? Estimates range from about two dozen up to about two hundred; he even turns up on lists of suspects for the true identity of Jack the Ripper.

Given that his usual habit was to kill people he knew, not just random strangers, it seems likely that the real number is *probably* closer to two dozen, but there's no way to tell. It's entirely possible that the murders of his friends, family, and employees are simply the ones that people were able to find out about. Stabbing several prostitutes to death, as Jack the Ripper did, wasn't exactly his style—but hey, he would have been on vacation at the time! His whereabouts in the time the Ripper was active are generally unknown, but in that period, Chicago does seem to have been his home base.

Even what records we have of him only complicate things further—his 1870 census lists little Herman W. Mudgett (his given name) as nine years old. When the census man came again in 1880, Mudgett was living in the home of his wife, Clara, with her parents and their four-month-old son, Robert, and gave his age as twenty two. Either he was lying, or he had pulled off the impressive trick of aging thirteen years in only a decade.

The marriage to Clara was a short one—according to some accounts, he never even met his son until years later (though the census records indicate otherwise). Shortly after the census was taken, he left the farm in New Hampshire to study medicine at the University of Michigan.

Most who have written about Holmes seem not to know it, but that particular university was a notorious hub for body snatching. Of course, most medical schools had a reputation for being involved in grave robbing in those days. And most refused to apologize. One senior official at the University of Louisville said, "We must have bodies. You cannot make doctors without them." But even in this environment, the University of Michigan seemed to make the news a lot for being caught purchasing bodies. Even when the market for bodies died in Chicago after the city began turning over paupers' bodies to the medical schools, grave robbing remained a problem in the city because there was still such a strong market in Ann Arbor. Chicago bodies continued to be dug up and sent on trains to Michigan in barrels labeled "kerosene" or "poultry."

A decade later, when Holmes's crimes came to light, one classmate, John Madden, wrote to the *Journal of the American Medical Association* to say what he remembered. "[Holmes] seemed to take a good deal of pleasure in the uncanny things of the dissection room," he wrote. "One afternoon's conversation with him I remember distinctly. He talked a great deal about what he had done in the dissecting room with what appeared to me at the time unnecessary gusto, and told me that the professor of anatomy was to permit him to take the body of an infant home with him for dissection during the spring vacation. I asked where he would find a place to carry on his work without offending his neighbors, and he replied with something to the effect that he 'would find a place.'"

Though Holmes listed Michigan as his home state in the university yearbook, going home for vacation may have still meant a trip back to New Hampshire. It's frightening to imagine Holmes traveling across the country with the rotten, stinking corpse of a baby among his luggage, eagerly awaiting the moment when he could take the body to the barn to carve it up.

Around 1884, Holmes arrived in Chicago, where he wooed and married a woman in Wilmette, in the north suburbs (a house he shared with her was still standing until the late 1990s). At the same time, he took a job far away from Wilmette in Englewood, then still a suburb of Chicago (which has since been absorbed into the city proper). There, he worked in a pharmacy run by Dr. and Mrs. Holton. In no time, he had become the owner—some believe that he accomplished this by killing Dr. and Mrs. Holton. In any case, he came to work in May of 1884, and in August of the next year the sign bearing the name E. S. HOLTON was lowered to the ground and replaced with one bearing the name H. H. HOLMES.

Thus began a ten-year flurry of activity for Holmes—simply reading a list of his various activities is enough to make the head spin. He was involved in one scheme after another, operating buildings all over the city and carrying on affairs with a number of women at once (marrying at least two of them in the process— by the time of his death, he had at least four wives, three of whom were still alive). In addition to the pharmacy in the south suburbs and the wife in the north suburbs, he was involved in a scheme to create a new kind of gas, forming a glass-bending company and building a factory to house it, running a candy shop near Wicker Park, operating a cigar company, forming a jewelry company, and running the ABC Copier Company from an office in the Loop.

Every time more research is done on Holmes, more business plans and schemes seem to be uncovered.

But the most famous of them all concerned the property he bought across the street from Holton's pharmacy. When Holmes bought it, it was a little lot containing trees and a cottage. The trees were cut down, the cottage was moved, and construction began on a building that Holmes would call the World's Fair Hotel.

The rest of the world would come to know it by another name: The Murder Castle.

The ground floor of the hulking building was like most others in the neighborhood—a block of retail shops. Holmes operated another drugstore here, and a restaurant, jewelry shop, tinsmith, and candy shop soon moved into the spots fronting Wallace Street. The second and third floors were said to be apartments to house visitors who came to Chicago for the 1893 World's Fair, which took place just down the road.

It's difficult today to overstate just what a big deal the World's Fair was. With hundreds of temporary buildings, the "White City" of the fairgrounds was the pride of the nation—a few of the buildings were among the largest in the world. The midway was crowned by a massive Ferris wheel (the large one currently at Navy Pier is a one-third-size replica). Here, Eadweard Muybridge offered his Zoopraxigraphical Hall, where he projected moving images of animals in motion against the wall, making it for all intents and purposes the first paid-movie theater in the world (it was a complete flop). For many fair patrons, the lighted buildings were their first glimpse of an electric light bulb. For all comers, the technology and ideas presented at the fair made it something of a preview of the coming twentieth century. There were twenty-seven million paid admissions—roughly equivalent to half the population of the United States at the time.

And just down 63rd Street, Holmes's hotel was waiting.

Really, to call it a hotel at all is something of a misnomer—it seems to have been more of a short-term apartment building than a hotel in the modern sense. Much of the second and third floors were given to offices; the residential rooms seem largely to have been occupied by people who lived there for the entire summer. But it's difficult to imagine that he would have built it in the way that he did just to kill a few people. Some of the space on the second floor, in particular, was given to rooms that the newspapers would eventually give such lurid names as "The Dark Room," "The Hanging Secret Chamber," "The Maze," "The Death Chute," "The Dummy Elevator for Lowering Bodies," "The Black Closet," "The Asphyxiation Chamber," "The Gas Chamber," and "The Room of the Three Corpses."

Indeed, the building had everything Holmes could need to kill a person. There was a gas chamber rigged with gas lines that he could control from his own private apartment. The "asphyxiation chamber" was a soundproof, airtight vault where people could be shut up for days at a time until succumbing to starvation or suffocation. When it was first under construction, Holmes asked one man to stand inside the chamber and scream as loud as he could to demonstrate that it was soundproof. The man thought it odd at the time, but was chilled months later when he realized how lucky he was that Holmes had opened the door and let him out.

In the course of construction, Holmes made sure that no one besides himself and a couple of close associates (henchmen, most likely) knew about the actual design. Construction workers would be hired for a week, then let go without pay and replaced with another crew, so that each worker knew only a little about the inner workings and design of the building.

Contrary to popular belief, though, the police knew about the building—and its secret chambers—before the World's Fair even started. And so did the public at large—it had actually been written up in the *Chicago Tribune* in early 1893.

Holmes, it seems, had purchased a lot of furniture on credit, but never paid a dime for it. The creditors obtained warrants to search the "castle," but turned up empty until an employee offered to show them where the furniture was being kept in exchange for fifty dollars. For this fee, he showed them a secret chamber in between the first and second floors where the furniture was being stashed. As they carted it away, he offered to show them more for another fifty dollars. This offer was refused; it's sobering to imagine what he might have shown them.

This encounter was detailed in the press. But no one thought he was using the secret rooms for anything more sinister than hiding stolen furniture—even though friends of Holmes, his employees, and their families had already begun to disappear.

While most serial killers tend to pick one sort of person to kill again and again, and usually use the same method over and over, Holmes is known to have killed men, women, and children in the course of his career, and by a variety of different methods.

Also, unlike most serial killers, his victims don't appear to be random. In many cases, they were murders that he planned out for months—often with the eventual goal of collecting insurance money. Again and again, as he took on new employees and wives, he would meet with their families to talk about life insurance—he would offer to buy them a policy, and pay the premiums himself, provided that he was one of the eventual benefactors. Then, sure enough, a few months after the ink was dry, they would disappear. Holmes would sometimes make money twice—by taking the insurance money, and by selling the bones to Charles Chappel, a skeleton "articulator" who sold articulated skeletons to medical schools.

All over, his friends, lovers, and employees vanished. Julia Connor, a woman he had stolen from her husband, Ned, vanished along with her daughter, Pearl. Minnie Williams, one of Holmes's many wives, vanished in 1893, shortly after her sister Anna also vanished. Emeline Cigrand, a stenographer in Holmes's employ, disappeared. So did Emily Van Tassel, an employee at a candy store he ran near Wicker Park under the name Frank Wild.

When the World's Fair ended, Holmes wandered down to Texas intending to build another castle on land owned by Minnie Williams but soon abandoned the enterprise and then found himself thrown in jail for a brief period in St. Louis. There, he struck up an acquaintance with one Marion Hedgepeth, a cellmate. For reasons that continue to baffle, Holmes told Hedgepeth all about his various insurance swindles—including his plans to murder his partner, Benjamin Pitezel, for the insurance money. When Hedgepeth told the police everything, he may have just been making it up to gain favor with the authorities—but he happened to be right about what Holmes had in mind.

After his release, Holmes suggested a scheme to Pitezel: they would go to Philadelphia, find a body that looked about like Pitezel, spray acid on the face to disguise the features, and say that he'd died in an explosion and collect the insurance money. Since Pitezel is known to have been a close enough confidant of Holmes that it's impossible to imagine he wasn't on to his schemes, if not an outright accomplice, one wonders just how dumb Pitezel had to be to go along on this plan.

But follow Holmes to Philadelphia he did, and rather than finding a look-alike body, Holmes simply killed Pitezel and left town. When Pitezel's body was discovered, it was buried in a pauper's grave under the name B. F. Perry. Holmes wrote to Fidelity Mutual to say that the man who'd been buried was really Benjamin Pitezel, whom they had insured for ten thousand dollars.

The insurance company had the body exhumed to make sure it was really him, and Holmes returned to Philadelphia where he and Alice, Pitezel's teenage daughter, identified the remains. He chilled the police (and presumably poor Alice) by casually taking a knife from his pocket and cutting a wart from the rotting remains, but the insurance company was satisfied that the remains were really Pitezel.

He collected the money for the widow, then told her that since Pitezel had owed him a lot of money, he was keeping most of it for himself—a jerk move if there ever was one.

Holmes then began to travel around North America along with fourteen-year-old Alice (who he was later accused of sleeping with), her sister Nellie, and their brother Howard. But the tip from Marion Hedgepeth helped the insurance company put two and two together: The body was Pitezel, but the death was no accident or suicide. They put the Pinkerton detectives on Holmes's trail, and he was eventually arrested (using an outstanding warrant from a Texas horse swindle) in Boston and taken to Philadelphia to stand trial for the murder of Benjamin Pitezel.

However, he no longer had the children in his custody. Holmes's story that he had turned them over to the missing Minnie Williams, who had taken them to England, satisfied no one, and detective Frank Geyer was put on the job of finding their true whereabouts. Geyer traveled throughout the continent, picking up Holmes's trail in rooming houses and hotels all across North America.

What he discovered was terrifying. Holmes had been traveling with three groups: one composed of himself and his latest wife, Georgiana (who thought his name was H. M. Howard); another composed of the three children; and the other composed of Mrs. Pitezel and two of her other children. None of the three groups knew that the other was nearby—the children thought their mother was miles away, though she was really in a hotel only blocks away. Mrs. Pitezel herself believed that her children were staying with a widow in Indianapolis, or with Minnie Williams in Detroit, at various times, though they were really a short walk from where she was being kept. That Holmes had coordinated these movements so skillfully awed even the district attorney at his trial—no military general was ever better organized.

Throughout the early parts of 1895, Geyer clung to a hope that he would find the children alive, but this was not to be. Alice and Nellie were found buried in a trunk underneath a cellar in Toronto. Having starved them to the point that they were no longer thinking straight, Holmes had allegedly induced them to hide in the trunk during a game of hide and seek, then inserted a gas hose to asphyxiate them. He had then chopped off Alice's feet (for fear that she could be identified by her club feet) and buried the trunk.

Later, the burned-up remains of Howard were found shoved up a chimney in Indiana.

He had gained no money from these killings and wouldn't have made any from killing Mrs. Pitezel and the other two (which he had planned to do, but never got around to). Some say that their murder was to keep people from testifying that Ben Pitezel was really dead. Others think that Holmes just liked to kill people.

As Holmes sat in a Philadelphia cell preparing for his trial, authorities in Chicago began to excavate the infamous Murder Castle.

Holmes had been out of the building for some time by then, but the basement yielded plenty of clues of dark work. There, they found plenty of means of disposing of human bodies—there was an acid pit where bodies could be dissolved, as well as a quicklime pit, which did the same thing, only not quite as quickly. A furnace was found, which was thought to have been used for cremations, and some human bones—allegedly those of Julia Connor and her daughter—were found buried beneath the ground, among several soup bones that Holmes had buried as a decoy, so that if bones were ever found, he could simply claim that they were animal bones, not human.

But two weeks of digging in the basement failed to yield any conclusive evidence. The quicklime was clearly unused, and it's hard to imagine just how much Holmes could have done in such a crowded building without arousing suspicion (though eager neighbors lined up to tell reporters that they'd been suspicious of Holmes all along and described in lurid detail chance meetings with Holmes during which, they were sure, they had narrowly escaped with their lives).

Indeed, one theory is that the entire basement of the castle was a decoy. Holmes had certainly buried a few soup bones to muddy the trail, and, since the *Tribune* had published a story about the building being full of secret passages and hidden rooms, he clearly expected that the building might be searched one day, and would have planned accordingly. While the police were busy with the castle, Patrick Quinlan, a janitor who was often described as Holmes's right-hand man, went to the North Side, where Holmes was in possession of a two-story house (where Minnie had briefly lived) in the rear of a shoddily built one-story building that he said was a glass-bending factory. The building fronted nothing but the Northwest line railroad and was surrounded by vacant lots and tenements occupied by immigrants who spoke only Polish. According to neighbors, while the building was in operation, trucks would arrive to unload a mysterious cargo that would be loaded back into the truck the same day.

While the police were at the castle, Quinlan had been seen carting away load after load of garbage. A few weeks later, when police finally learned of the building, all they found was rubble, some papers signed by Quinlan and Holmes (many related to the ABC Copier Company that Holmes had operated in the Loop), some ashes, and plans indicating that there had recently been a massive furnace spanning the whole length of the building. It would have been perfectly large enough to handle cremations, and police announced that if Holmes had been killing people, he had likely destroyed the evidence here. That a few of his victims had lived near the site was hard to overlook as well.

But this was only one theory to explain all the disappearances. It was apparent that Holmes had killed several people, including the Pitezel children, but some detectives and reporters were baffled as to his motives. Why would he have killed the children? There was no financial motive for him to do so, after all. At the time, the idea that he might have simply been killing for fun, or for sexual gratification, would have seemed absurd to people. When Patrick Quinlan was extensively questioned by the police, a newspaper cried that the whole investigation had gotten out of hand, and demanded that Quinlan be released. Released he was, and a couple of years later he tried (unsuccessfully) to sue the police for having questioned him at all.

And though some expressed shock that a man could be accused of so much for which he had no financial motive, most modern researchers believe that Holmes certainly killed the Pitezel children—as well as dozens, perhaps hundreds, of others. By many estimates, he was not just the first serial killer in the United States, but the most prolific as well.

As for the castle itself, a massive fire destroyed what little evidence there was in August of 1895. In fall of that year, the charred remains of the second and third floors were torn down and rebuilt. The first story and basement, with the new additions, continued to stand on 63rd Street until the late 1930s, when they were razed to make way for a post office. Some say that parts of the basement are still present below the office, and elderly people who grew up in the neighborhood tell stories of being superstitious about the old building long after its history had been forgotten.

As for Holmes himself, he was found guilty of a single murder—that of Benjamin Pitezel, and set about writing his notorious confession,[4] for which he was well paid. Over the course of his incarceration, he grew a beard and told anyone who would listen that his physical form was changing. His face was becoming more elongated, and he was gradually beginning to take the shape of the devil himself.

He was hanged in May of 1896, confessing on the scaffold that he had killed two people (both as a result of performing "illegal operations"—abortions—on them). At his request, he was buried in a massive block of cement to protect his own body from his fellow body snatchers.

Shortly thereafter, beginning just before his hanging and continuing for some months after it, people associated with the trial that damned Holmes began to die. Over the years, more than thirty people associated with Holmes and the trial came into misfortune ranging from personal setbacks to suicide. Patrick Quinlan wrote a note saying, "I could not sleep" and killed himself at his Michigan farm. Marion Hedgepeth was shot to death in Chicago and languished in the morgue for six weeks before being buried in a pauper's grave. The jailer shot himself. The jury foreman was electrocuted. The office of the insurance agent who pressed charges against Holmes caught fire.

Some say that Holmes was getting revenge from beyond the grave.

---

4 The most famous line from his confession, "I was born with the devil in me," is absent from the confession as published in the *Inquirer.* That section—widely quoted at the time in regional papers—came from *The Philadelphia North American,* which claimed to have seen advance copies of the *Inquirer* confession. The confession contained similar ideas, but not that actual line.

Others suggest that it may be more reasonable simply to believe that Holmes had faked his death and was getting his revenge in person.

The beard (which was shaved just before the execution) and the stories that his facial features were changing may have been a ruse to confuse anyone who noticed that he looked a bit different on the scaffold, and the block of cement is especially odd. Holmes was not a man who believed that human remains were sacred by any means—but the cement certainly guarded his remains against anyone who wanted to dig up the remains to establish that it was truly him in that grave. Nearly every reporter or doctor who spoke to him in prison toward the end noted that he looked nothing like his pictures.

Even now, efforts are being made to have the body exhumed to see if the monster of 63rd Street's career truly ended in 1896, or if he had lived to kill again and again. He would have been an old man—but not *too* old—when another World's Fair came to Chicago in 1933.

CHAPTER 10

George Pullman
Palace Car Patriarch

There are, as you can see, plenty of stories about Gilded Age robber barons who have gone down in history as jerks. But one guy was such a jerk that his family went to extreme lengths to protect him from angry employees—even after his death.

George Pullman was a bit of a visionary—he became rich off of his own inventions, and then dreamed up a model city for the workers in his factories. The nineteenth century was an age of utopian thinking. But Pullman's ideals (and their failures) would come into a deadly clash with the ideals of some of his workers and their opponents in one of the deadliest labor riots in American history, and Pullman wound up so hated by his employees that the family spent a ton of money to protect his remains—allegedly from vengeful employees—after his death

Pullman's model town drew a lot of praise in its day—while plenty of factories in those days set their employees up in shanties and paid them only in credit to the company store (where everything was overpriced), Pullman built a whole town with excellent housing, including its own hotel and recreational facilities. But a code of conduct for residents was strictly enforced. No one was allowed to drink in town (except for Pullman and his guests, who could drink at the hotel), and in 1893, when an economic depression hit, as they tended to do every few years, Pullman slashed the wages of his employees—but didn't lower their rent.

This, of course, caused trouble that would stain his legacy forever.

Born in New York in 1831, Pullman came to Chicago as a young man intending to supervise the building of Chicago's first sewer system. When it became clear that Chicago was built on land that was too low-lying and damp, it was determined that the city needed to be raised up about eight feet before sewers could be installed.

Pullman, using a technique his father had taught him, supervised the raising up of several buildings. The foundation for a building would be dug out, and several jacks were placed beneath it, with one worker manning each jack. At a given signal, each man would turn the jack a quarter turn, raising the building up just a little.

By this method, it was said, workers were able to raise a crowded hotel up several feet without anyone inside noticing what was happening. This almost had to have been an exaggeration; surely they must have at least noticed a man blowing a whistle over and over again outside.

But it's certainly no exaggeration to say that raising up the Tremont House gave Pullman a heck of a reputation. He further cemented his fame by developing the "Pullman sleeper," a sort of luxury railroad car that was also known as a "palace car" and which gained national attention when Pullman arranged to use one of them to transport the body of Abraham Lincoln from Washington, D.C., to Springfield during the mini "tour" the body took, stopping in every major city along the way so that people could pay their respects to the fallen president. Upwardly mobile people everywhere raced to enjoy the same comfort the corpse had enjoyed.

Soon, Pullman was launching entire luxury trains—one version was like a hotel on wheels, and another was themed around serving luxury cuisine to passengers. Riding a train had previously been a long, uncomfortable experience for many people. Riding a Pullman train was like going to a resort, with first-class service provided by recently freed slaves who found with the Pullman company their first paying jobs.

All of this made Pullman fabulously wealthy, and in 1880 he bought four thousand acres of land fourteen miles south of Chicago to build the town of Pullman, a model city for his factory workers. Though he would later raise the ire of socialists, his model town

The Hotel Florence in Pullman
CHICAGO DAILY NEWS

was really a sort of socialist utopian "worker's paradise." It had fine housing, stores, churches, parks, and theaters for his workers.

But Pullman didn't do all of this out of the goodness of his heart—he intended to make money off of the town. Lots of it.

This plot of land was not yet a part of Chicago, meaning that Pullman could effectively run the town all on his own as a sort of supreme dictator. It was remarked that no figurehead in Europe had more power than Pullman did over his employees, many of whom were now also his tenants. When you live in a privately owned town, effectively as a twenty-four-hour employee, you give up most of your constitutional rights and have to live by the company's rules.

Pullman refused to allow public speeches or meetings. Only approved denominations could rent the church (and none of them did). Workers could be evicted and fired for not upholding the standards of cleanliness in their homes that Pullman expected. One worker supposedly wrote, "We are born in a Pullman house, fed from Pullman shops, taught in the Pullman school, catechized in the Pullman Church, and when we die we shall go to the Pullman Hell."

Indeed, though people throughout the world looked at Pullman as a benevolent visionary, his workers often seemed to be living out a Bruce Springsteen song about working-class alienation. They were strictly divided by class. Executives lived in ten-room houses. Managers got smaller frame houses. Skilled laborers with families were put into tight, red-bricked row houses, and single men were put up in crowded boarding houses and pre-planned slums. The centerpiece of the town, the dazzling Hotel Florence, was off-limits to most workers.

When the City of Chicago began annexing land to the south of the city proper in 1889, Pullman lost a lot of his control over the town and how it was run. He was hit a lot harder, though, by the depression that came in the 1890s.

When we think of "The Depression" now, our thoughts go strictly to the 1930s. But the reason they began to call that era "The Great Depression" was to distinguish it from the many *other* depressions and panics that had come up throughout the nineteenth century. The worst of them may have been The Panic of 1893.

In that year, concerns about the economy led people to pull their money from the banks (in those pre-FDIC days, if the bank failed, your money went with it). The federally mandated minimum amount of gold in federal reserves was reached, and bank notes could no longer be exchanged for actual gold, as they had been before. Fifteen thousand companies went bankrupt, five hundred banks failed. Unemployment approached 20 percent. Newly built mansions were abandoned (according to historian Charles Hoffman, these abandoned Victorians that rotted away in the middle of handsome towns forever fixed in our minds the popular image of a haunted house).

Naturally, in such an economic climate, people were less likely to spend extra money on luxury travel. The Pullman Company was hit hard, and Pullman doesn't really seem to have planned for a rainy day.

To make up for his losses, Pullman appeared to take things out on his employees. He laid many workers off (and, since many of them were also his tenants, this meant kicking them out of their houses) and wages were cut by as much as 50 percent. But he kept the price of rent on the housing right where it was.

In 1894, Pullman workers went on strike. This itself didn't hurt the company all that badly, really, but the American Railway Union, led by a young go-getter named Eugene Debs, began to boycott Pullman cars, knocking them off of railroads in twenty-seven states. This was trouble.

All over Illinois, as striking workers blocked trains, freight cars stood still. There was an ever-present fear that businessmen would be stranded in the city if suburban commuter trains were stopped. Debs, whom newspapers referred to as "Dictator Debs," urged people across the country to boycott Pullman trains.

In an "appeal to the public" that Debs was forced to write from the Cook County Jail after being arrested, he said, "The Pullman company makes the plea that it is asked of them that they shall run their works at a loss. The statement is absolutely false. . . . The Pullman Company has robbed its employees and an investigation would have disclosed a state of affairs which would have horrified the nation . . . it is notoriously true that the Pullman company pays its conductors and porters such paltry wages that they are obliged to depend on the public to support them. Yes, this rich and powerful corporation virtually compels the public to pay the wages of their sleeping car employees . . . shall the Pullman company have the support of the public in carrying out this hellish policy? Shall the public be a party to the starvation and degradation of these more than four thousand employees, men and women, whose only crime is that they ask living wages?"

While the papers generally took Pullman's side (this was less than a decade after they had crowed that the world was "safe for democracy" after the execution of the Haymarket anarchists), the public began to turn against Mr. Pullman himself. He came off looking like something of a jerk when he was cross-examined by the

United States Labor Commission at the end of the summer, when he stated that he had no right to give the employees money when he could have obtained their labor at a lower cost and given the money he saved to his stockholders, but had every right to take contracts to build cars for less money, knowing full well that he'd have to cut wages. In other words, he had every right to cut pay to his workers, but not to his stockholders. This may have seemed logical to many, but it didn't exactly win Mr. Pullman a lot of new fans.

Over the summer the strikes turned into riots. Train cars were overturned and shots were fired. And as more stories about the treatment of Pullman employees leaked out, one minister testified that one of his congregants, a Pullman employee, had been injured on the job in an "unavoidable accident," and after receiving inadequate medical care, he was only given his job back at a greatly reduced wage and charged rent for the time he was in the hospital, unable to earn wages at all.

Though Debs was not entirely successful, workers everywhere sided with the Pullman employees, and every day new "sympathy strikes" were announced.

The strike would eventually be settled, but not before twelve thousand federal marshals had to be called in. Thirteen strikers were killed, and the other strikers destroyed hundreds of thousands of dollars in public property. There were no real "winners" in the strikes; all of the major players became embittered by the whole affair. Debs became a socialist and ran for president as the Socialist Party candidate several times, even though he once had to do so from a prison cell. In 1912, he got 6 percent of the popular vote, a remarkable feat for a third-party candidate (in a four-man race, no less; most of the "progressive" vote that year went to Theodore Roosevelt's Bull Moose Party, which won Cook County on the strength of Chicago and came in second nationwide, defeating Taft and the Republicans but losing to Woodrow Wilson).

Pullman, too, became a bitter man. A commission found his town to be "un-American," and declared that his paternalistic attitude was at least partially to blame for the strike.

*Interior view of the attic apartment of one of Pull-
man's employee-tenants*
CHICAGO DAILY NEWS

He survived for barely three more years, and many of his
friends said that the Debs-led strike had given him an illness from
which he never quite recovered. He began to suffer from heart ail-
ments, and he died in his bedroom in 1897. His position as head
of the company was taken over by Robert Todd Lincoln, whose
father's body had made the sleeping cars famous.

He remained unpopular with workers, and it may have been
this that led his family to take great precautions to protect his
remains after his death (though the fact that the body of A. T.
Stewart, merchant prince of New York, had been stolen and held
for ransom was surely on their minds, as well).

In the Pullman plot at Graceland, workers dug an eight-foot
pit, the bottom eighteen inches of which was filled with concrete
reinforced by metal bars. The coffin, once lowered inside, was
wrapped in tarpaper and asphalt. The already-added cement was
heated and more cement was poured on, making it into one huge
mass of stone, guarded by eight heavy-steel rails bolted together
by iron rods.

The underground fortress was judged to be impregnable—dynamite itself couldn't break in, let alone a lowly worm. "The body of George M. Pullman," the *Tribune* wrote, "will lie undisturbed as long as time shall last. None of the Egyptian monarchs, supposedly resting under the ponderous weight of the pyramids, sleeps more secure from the encroachment of the living world than does the sleeping car magnate in his grave at Graceland." It's likely that if someone managed to break in today, the body would be in perfect condition, perhaps even still bearing his Colonel Sanders–like goatee.

Today, it's difficult to pass judgment on Old Mr. Pullman. His record as an employer has a few glaring black marks, but he generally compares favorably with other employers of his era, when equitable treatment was seen as the gift of a kindly employer, not the right of the employees.

Pullman had lived to see the day in 1896 when, despite the unrest and bad publicity he and the town had received two years earlier, it was voted "The World's Most Perfect Town" by the jury of the International Hygienic and Pharmaceutical Exposition, but, obviously, it wasn't an honor that everyone agreed with, and in the twentieth century the land was annexed and became just a neighborhood in Chicago, one that fell into decline with much of the rest of the South Side. But the Hotel Florence still towers over it, and the neighborhood is undergoing a rapid process of gentrification.

CHAPTER 11

Kitty Adams
Terror of State Street

Those of us who spend our lives re-telling stories of crime and disasters often notice a curious phenomenon: People may drop their jaws or cringe a bit when we talk of people dying gruesome deaths, but you'll always get a more profound and vocal reaction from a crowd if you mention a dead dog or horse.

Hence, the easiest way to persuade people that Mrs. Kitty Adams, once known as the "Terror of State Street" was a real jerk was to mention that once, while involved in a scuffle with the driver of a scavenger wagon, she intimidated the driver by pulling a razor from her cleavage and cutting a six-inch gash into the side of his horse.

This was only one of hundreds of scuffles Kitty started in her career on the Near South Side. By some estimates, she was guilty of a robbery roughly every three days over the course of several years.

Growth for Chicago was always a double-edged sword. When construction was hot and the train fares were low, Chicago was immeasurably enriched by the hundreds of thousands who came to town to take advantage of the boom. But plenty of drifters and lowlifes came, too.

In the late 1850s, most of the crime and vice was confined to a single neighborhood: The Sands, the beachfront portion of the Near North Side. But after the Great Chicago Fire destroyed most of downtown, red-light districts throughout the area began to thrive as the city, now growing faster than ever, attracted count-less vagrants. While Captain Streeter built up his own shanty town north of The Loop, the southern end of downtown thrived on its own. Lowdown brothels, saloons, and parlors covered State

Street, and it was estimated that in 1885 there were five hundred opium dens in the city.

Panel houses, hotels "of ill repute" with hidden panels in which thieves could hide and rob the customers in their sleep, sprung up all through the town. In the early 1890s, police estimated that a million-and-a-half dollars worth of cash and goods had been stolen from panel house customers in a single year.

In the early 1890s, ground zero for crime and vice was a little neighborhood called Hell's Half Acre, off State Street just below Polk. According to Clifton Wooldridge, a police officer who patrolled the district and later wrote a memoir (in which he referred to himself in the third person), "it was a continual scene of revelry, debauchery, depravity, and every sin and crime in the blood-stained catalogue of vice. Its crimes, sad to relate, were of the lowest and vilest nature. The most defiant and reckless characters that ever menaced society made this place their home . . . it was a hotbed of crime and a cesspool of vice . . . every house was a saloon or barber shop or house of ill-fame." One wonders why he seemed to put barbershops in the same category as saloons and houses of ill-fame, but it's a safe bet that barbershops in the neighborhood were doing a lot more than cutting hair.

And Hell's Half Acre was only one little sub-neighborhood of the long strip of State Street, from Van Buren to 22nd Street, that Wooldridge called Satan's Mile. Bawdy houses and saloons were open all night and were in plentiful supply all down the street. "These places," said Wooldridge, "were the resort of the desperate burglars, thieves and sure-thing gamblers. . . . [the alleys were] frequently selected by footpads, highwaymen, strong-arm women and robbers."

The worst of these strong-arm women of Satan's Mile may have been Kitty Adams, the Terror of State Street. Adams came to town in the 1880s as the wife of George Shine, a pickpocket, and made a name for herself with her skills with a razor blade, which she learned to wield while living in a brothel. Stories of her prowess with it spread through the town; some say that she once pulled

Scenes from the saloons around State Street

the razor from her cleavage and cut off the ears of one of her lovers (though the fact that said lover was black made as much scandal as any other part of the story).

And this was all before she took up life as a "footpad," a thief who specialized in robbing pedestrians (not unlike the current term, "mugger"), and became known as the leader of "a lot of harpies who prowl about the downtown districts late at night," as the *Tribune* put it. Using her razor, she was estimated to have committed some seven hundred robberies between 1886 and 1893, when she was finally sent to prison in Joliet. It had been hard to put her into prison strictly because few men were willing to go into court and testify that they'd been robbed by a woman—or that they'd even been in Satan's Mile to start with.

In fact, in one case, the judge actually ruled that it was the victim's fault just for being in the neighborhood.

A man named Mr. Whitney had been walking the streets when Kitty and her partner-in-crime, one Jennie Clark, spied him. "There's a guy with rocks," Kitty said. "Let's nab him."

Each of them walked along one side of the man, and one of them threw an arm around his chin to hold him while her free hand covered his mouth so that no one could hear him cry "police." The other skillfully emptied the man's vest and pant pockets to take him for every cent he had—about five dollars in all.

All of this was done in front of numerous witnesses, and Detective Wooldridge was right nearby. He was able to catch Kitty and Jennie before they could get to a hiding place and booked them for robbery at the Harrison Street station.

At the trial, Judge Goggin, who dealt with Adams fairly often and seemed surprisingly comfortable using street slang, called them "poor unfortunates" and proceeded to lecture the victim.

"This old steamboat," he said, as he glared at Mr. Whitney from the bench, "was paddling down that street full of whiskey. He hitched onto these two barges and got what he was looking for. After towing them awhile he wanted to cut loose and now he kicks because he thinks their toll charges were exorbitant . . . it

Common among the saloons were "panel houses," where people would hide behind a panel to steal from people in the rooms.

served the old duck right to lose his money. I am sorry that he did not have more money to lose. White whiskers ought to know better than to be on that street so late at night. Why, I am a property-owner down that way and do you think I would trust my life there at midnight? No, not for $20."

And all of this was *after* it became known that Kitty Adams had lied her way into getting a pardon from the governor to get out of her last jail sentence.

By the early 1890s, it would be polite to say that Kitty had "outgrown the brothel." The *Chicago Herald* simply said, "Six years ago the Adams woman was exceptionally handsome . . . dissipation has dimmed her beauty." The same paper marveled that, "as a pickpocket she is tremendously expert; it is nothing for her to take from the inside pocket of her victim's waistcoat his pocketbook, remove the contents and replace the same without detection. To remove a ring from his finger without his knowl-edge is one of her stronger points, while shirt studs fall into her hands as if by magic."

While Kitty was in prison serving a ten-month sentence in 1893, Jennie Clark petitioned the governor to let her out of jail on the grounds that she was dying of consumption (tuberculosis), and wouldn't survive a week.

Kitty was summarily brought before the board of pardons, where they looked at her decayed, bleeding gums and watched, disgusted, as she coughed up blood. Convinced that she'd never live long enough to rob another man, her pardon was granted.

The police were indignant. The *Tribune* said, "Governor John P. Altgeld should have seen the expression of disgust on the face of the Chicago police yesterday when they heard he had par-doned Kitty Adams from the bridewell (prison). Their language was almost strong enough to reach him even in the Gubernatorial chair at Springfield . . . for Kitty Adams is probably the toughest proposition in the way of a female criminal that the Chicago police ever encountered. She has been arrested by the officers an average of fifty-two times a year for the last six years."

This does not make Kitty look quite as sharp a robber as she was made out to be. Do some quick math, and you find that, though she was adept at keeping out of jail after being caught, she was arrested roughly half the times she robbed a person.

The prison officials, for their part, certainly hadn't noticed that she was sick. The only "consumption" noticed in her, they said, was "a wholesale consumption of food."

Naturally, she quickly recovered and went right back to her old tricks. It was quite certain, a paper said, that Kitty had "about as sound a pair of lungs as anybody who has been in [police] clutches recently."

"We have heard lately, said a Central Station man, "that Kitty has been having hemorrhages of the lungs. But she's only been picking her teeth and expectorating blood, an old trick of criminals to gain sympathy . . . she's a hard bird to cage."

Luckily for the police, she wasn't *impossible* to cage. Two years later, they finally made a charge stick on her, and she was sent to prison in Joliet. Writing a few years later, Wooldridge said, "She was sentenced . . . for an indefinite term, and it is not likely she will get out on the same pretense which liberated her before."

He was right, and Kitty could have learned a thing or two from the Boy Who Cried Wolf. While serving that indefinite sentence, she caught tuberculosis for real. No pardon was forthcoming this time, and she died in prison.

CHAPTER 12

Adolph Luetgert
Sausage King of Chicago

Every now and then when I'm running a tour in Chicago, traffic will force us onto Diversey Street, where we'll pass by the condos that have been built into the old sausage factory where Adolph Luetgert allegedly killed his wife and dissolved the body in a sausage curing vat.

It's a hard story to tell to a group of people. Once you've mentioned a sausage factory at all on a crime tour, any ending to the story that doesn't involve someone actually being ground into sausage and sold to unsuspecting neighbors is bound to be a bit anticlimactic.

Indeed, as soon as you say *sausage,* people start to murmur.

"I bet I know where this is going!" someone will say.

People who think all the stories I'm telling are made up are especially smug. "We heard the same story on that tour in New Orleans, didn't we, Ed?" a woman might say to her husband. "About the woman who got ground into sausage?"

"I thought that happened in a sausage factory on Clybourne," another will say.

Indeed, there are a *lot* of stories out there—some of which are even true—about people getting ground up and sold as sausage.

But Louisa Luetgert wasn't one of them.

Exactly what Adolph Luetgert did to his wife, Louisa, has never been firmly established, really, but one thing we know for sure is that he didn't actually go so far as to grind her into sausage. The sausage factory was not in operation at the time she disappeared.

Still, he did murder her—and when word went around that some human remains had been found in the sausage curing vats, you can probably imagine what happened to sausage sales in the city.

Heck, even back in the 1890s, when rumors of the story first began to circulate, a jump-rope rhyme became common throughout the North Side:

> Old Man Luetgert made sausage out of his wife
> he turned on the steam
> she began to scream
> there'll be a hot time in the old town tonight!

Alas, though the jump-rope rhyme is said to survive among Bucktown area children to this day, no one was ever actually tricked into eating Louisa Links. Adolph Luetgert may have been a jerk, but he was not the kind of guy who went around making people eat dead humans.

Of course, if that's the best you can say about someone, it's not saying much.

But today, more than a century after Luetgert was convicted, the mystery is still considered to be unsolved by many. Was Louisa murdered, melted down, and washed away into the Chicago River, or did she just run off to get away from her jerk of a husband?

The investigation into his wife's disappearance in 1897 was a landmark case in the development of forensics, and for a time the case was billed (like so many others) as the Crime of the Century.

In 1871, just after the Great Chicago Fire, Adolph Luetgert came to Chicago as a twenty-six-year-old man with exactly three cents in his pocket and was industrious enough to open a grocery store the next year. It may have been here that he committed his first murder.

In 1879, police found the lifeless body of local no-goodnik Hugh McGowan in the alley behind a saloon Luetgert was operating on Clybourne. He looked, at a glance, as though he had simply been killed in a drunken brawl (a leading cause of death in early Chicago), but he turned out to have been choked to death with a wad of chewing tobacco. Police could prove nothing, but the best theory they could come up with was that McGowan had spat a

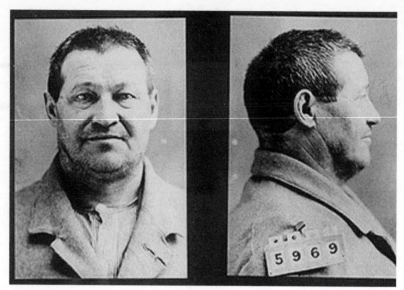

Luetgert's mug shot
COOK COUNTY

wad of tobacco on Luetgert's sidewalk, and Luetgert, a gigantic man compared to the wiry McGowan, had gripped his head in a hammerlock and shoved an enormous plug of tobacco right into his throat, then left him to choke to death in the alley. But in those days before Luetgert's DNA could have been found in McGowan's body, there was no hard evidence on which he could be held.

No one ever claimed that Luetgert was the sort of guy who always had a smile for everyone. He was a big and imposing man—more than six feet tall, and well north of two hundred pounds. As the *Tribune* described him, "He has the massive frame and the face of those who work in slaughter houses, and to whom the smell of blood and fresh meat is healthful . . . he has huge, red hands that are thick with fat, and a neck like an Egyptian column, that, when he puts back his head, wrinkles up in folds below his skull."

When his first wife died while she was pregnant in 1881, neighbors wondered if Adolph and his temper had something to do with it.

Now single, Adolph married the much younger Louisa Bicknese and opened his first sausage factory. As a wedding gift, he gave her a massive, fourteen-carat diamond ring with her initials engraved on the inside of the band.

He built himself a huge new factory on Diversey Street, towering above the miniscule buildings of the neighborhood like a grimy palace in a little village, with a three-story house on the grounds where the two of them would live. The house was nice, but one suspects that Louisa probably wasn't exactly content there. An enormous husband with a bad temper and the smell of the sausage factory rolling into the windows—just what every young wife dreams of.

If there was a honeymoon period at all, it was a brief one—Adolph and Louisa's arguments were the talk of the neighborhood. Everyone could hear them shouting at each other, and rumors went around that he was even beating her. Certainly she was no match for him. Louisa was a slight woman of small frame, a dwarf compared to the hulking Adolph. The newspapers wrote that she "served him like a slave."

Everyone figured it was for the best when Adolph moved out of the house and into the factory, where he set himself up a simple, forty-five-square-foot windowless apartment with all he needed: a bed, a dresser, and two shelves. When police eventually searched it, they found one of the shelves stocked with liquor, and the other with provisions: a half-eaten pound cake and an ivory-handled pistol. A sign on the wall read, THIS ROOM FOR MR. LUETGERT ONLY.

But few were the nights when he was the only one in the tiny room. He was often seen "entertaining" a wealthy widow, a young servant, and even, it was said, one of Louisa's own nieces, among others.

In the spring of 1897, the factory was shut down for renovations. Luetgert already considered himself the Sausage King of Chicago and had set his sights on taking his operation worldwide. It was this ambition that had led to many of the fights with Louisa—expanding his operations was an expensive procedure, and, naturally, money had to be raised. He had taken out huge sums in loans. When the loans began to fall through, and the dreams of expansion began to collapse, both of them began to worry that the entire operation would soon be foreclosed on. Even with Adolph out of the house most of the time, the fights got louder and more frequent.

It was in early summer that neighbors realized they hadn't seen Louisa around in a while.

Her two sons, Louis and Elmer, were curious as to where their mother had gotten to as well. One night they had been talking to her about the circus, and the next morning she was simply gone. Their father told them that she had gone off to visit relatives in Kenosha.

After some time passed and their mother didn't return, the boys got suspicious—after all, no one could possibly stay in Kenosha for *that* long. The two turned into juvenile detectives, wandering the neighborhood asking if anyone had seen their mother. This naturally alerted the neighbors, and Adolph dropped the charade and went to the police station to report his wife as a missing person.

The police told Adolph they'd look into it, but they suspected him immediately. None of Louisa's relatives, in Kenosha or elsewhere, claimed to have seen her, and all of the neighbors who were questioned confirmed that she and Adolph had been known for their quarrels. One remembered chatting happily with her the night she was last seen alive—she certainly hadn't *seemed* as though she was about to run away.

Several others noticed that there seemed to be some activity in the factory that night. One workman noted that one of the basement boilers and steam works had been turned on—and that Adolph had recently had more than fifty pounds of arsenic delivered to the factory, along with three hundred pounds of potash. It was an odd shipment for a factory that wasn't doing anything.

That same watchman said that the next morning, he had found the sausage curing vat in the basement overflowing with a greasy red substance that had spread onto the floor. A chair was set up nearby for no particular reason.

It wasn't hard to put the pieces together—mixing arsenic and potash into a steaming vat would create a caustic brew that could boil right through a body. A body stirred about in such a mixture would be completely dissolved in a couple of hours.

The investigation was not without some bizarre drama. At one point, Adolph angrily accused the police of hiring "ghosts." Apparently, he had seen Louisa's ghost around the neighborhood, and believed that the police had hired someone to dress up as Louisa to scare him into confessing.

Though he insisted that Louisa had simply run away, police began a thorough investigation of the factory and made two discoveries in the sausage vat: a small fragment of bone, and a ring bearing the initials L. L. Mysterious dark stains—the color of blood—were found in the bedroom and office. A man who lived nearby said he'd heard a woman scream the night Louisa was last seen.

Outside, in the gunk that filled the potholes of the unpaved road, police found some more clues—a false tooth, more bone fragments, a hairpin, and a corset stay. A fisherman casting lines from the Diversey Street Bridge reeled in some human hair—blonde, like Louisa's.

Adolph was placed under arrest and marched out of the factory, and rumors that he had killed his wife for sausage meat began to spread at once. Sausage sales plummeted.

The police couldn't establish the actual method by which Louisa was done in. The massive indictment covered just about every possibility—she may have been strangled, stabbed, bludgeoned, beaten, shot, or tied up and thrown alive into the gurgling vat where her body had been dissolved.

The trial began barely two months after the arrest and quickly became a bit of a circus. Though it seemed like an open-and-shut case, it really wasn't so simple. A few witnesses swore they'd seen Louisa wandering around in Kenosha, fifty miles north. And the defense insisted that the bone fragments were simply animal bones. Rumors swarmed that Louisa herself would be called as a surprise witness.

Meanwhile, Agatha Tosch, a local barmaid, had to take the stand and swear that she had never dressed up in a white sheet to scare Adolph into confessing. She did note, however, that one night in her bar, Adolph had been overheard saying, "I feel as if I could take my wife and . . ."

Here she was interrupted by Luetgert jumping to his feet to shout, "It's not true! It's a sham! It's not true!"

Shaken by the sight of Luetgert's rage, Mrs. Tosch never did complete her sentence. Later that same day, another witness, who identified the ring in the vat as Louisa's, spoke of seeing Adolph chase Louisa around the neighborhood with a revolver.

For months the trial slogged on, with the police and prosecution fairly certain that Luetgert had, in fact, murdered Louisa, but unable to prove that the witnesses who had seen her in Kenosha were wrong, or that any of the bones or blood found were of human origin. The jury was unable to reach a verdict, and a mistrial was called. Luetgert would sit in his cell for another month before the proceedings could be restarted.

The second trial dragged on even longer, and, since no dead body had been found, the prosecution tried a new "witness," Dr. George Dorsey, an anthropologist from The Field Museum.

It was the emerging science of forensics that finally doomed old man Luetgert. The first "experts" brought in to examine the bone fragments said that they may be human, but were just as likely animal bones, as the prosecution had insisted. And proving that the dark stains on the walls were human blood was not yet possible.

But Dorsey was able to make some shocking discoveries that made the case a landmark in the history of forensics.

Dorsey had determined, after a thorough examination, that the bones were human. They had certain characteristics, he said, which indicated that they could not be the bones of a pig, a sheep, a cow, or any other animal that would be found in a slaughterhouse. They were the bones, he said, of a single human body. The one found in the vat came from a human toe. The flesh around it had protected the bone from the caustic mixture just long enough for it to survive to be carried away by the outflow.

Another star witness was the memorably named Frank Odorofsky, a smoker from the sausage factory, who threw water on the defense's assumption that the mixture would have been too weak if it were left to boil uncovered. Odorofsky didn't speak English himself, but, through an interpreter and several bold gestures, told the story of how Adolph had ordered him to make up the sticky, foul-smelling "red slime" in the vat, even though the dust that flew up as he poured out the contents had burned his hands and face like live coals and ate into his skin like acid.

He testified that he had covered up the vat with a few loose doors, trapping the steam inside and making it far stronger than it would have been if left uncovered, and further related the tale that Adolph had offered him "a place for life" in exchange for cleaning up the slime that was leftover in the vat the next day. By then, red slime was everywhere in the basement. As Odorofsky shoveled it out, he said, he had seen bones and flesh mixed into the gunk. He was clearly disgusted with the gunk himself, which he described in German as "sleimisch," drawing out the word with such hisses that the audience in the courtroom needed no interpreter to know that the mixture he was describing was a gruesome one.

For the first time, Luetgert began to sweat. At various times during Odorofsky's testimony, he had appeared ready to jump up and start yelling at the jury. Privately, he growled that Odorofsky, and all of the other witnesses, were "a bunch of damned perjurers . . . it is plain to everybody that they have been too stupid to learn by heart everything the police have tried to teach them." With this to contend with, the defense finally put Luetgert on the stand, where, for the first time, he explained what he was doing with the caustic soda in the sausage vat that evening.

His four word testimony: "I was making soap."

No one quite bought this. Though sightings of Louisa continued to be reported, she never seemed to turn up. Rumors that she was on her way to Chicago from Michigan to appear as a surprise witness in the trial came to nothing.

No one back on the Near Northwest Side seemed to think Adolph was innocent. The lone exception was a man who demanded a meeting with the defense attorney, who insisted that they *must* get Adolph off the hook. "You see," he said, "you *must* do it or it will overcome me. I have a judgment against him for $39.85, and I don't see how I will collect it if they hang him!"

Finally, the jury retired to deliberate. Stories circulated about newspapers trying every kind of trick to bug the jury room to see what was going on—the trial had, by now, attracted international interest, and newspapers weren't about to let a little thing like the law beat their chances of getting the scoop.

But when the jury announced a guilty verdict, Luetgert laughed cynically. "She'll come back!" he roared. "Then you'll see what fools you've been!" By most accounts, he looked relieved just to be done with the trial. "It is a halfway verdict," he said. "I am satisfied."

Since the body was missing, leaving a bare sliver of reasonable doubt, Luetgert was sentenced to life in prison, not the gallows. He was taken to Joliet, where he spent the next two years raving that Louisa was still alive and visiting his cell. Some say that he was seeing ghosts. Rumors that Louisa was haunting the factory began to circulate—one police officer even reported chasing the ghost through the factory to the old sausage vat one night—and still float around occasionally today, now that the building has been converted into condos.[5]

Luetgert died in his cell two years later, and Louisa never reappeared.

---

5 Several accounts of the trial say that the building burned down in 1902. This is half true—there was a fire in 1902, but the building survived, and is still there today.

CHAPTER 13

"Bathhouse John" Coughlin
The Bard of the Levee

In the late nineteenth century, as the city made its rapid transition from being a Wild West outpost to a major city, two aldermen dominated the politics of the South Side "Levee" District, the home of the most notorious brothels and saloons in town: "Bathhouse John" Coughlin and "Hinky Dink" Kenna.

Both men probably qualify as jerks simply by being fabulously corrupt, but Bathhouse probably had the edge over old Hinky Dink for one simple reason: Hinky Dink never made people read his awful poetry, like Bathhouse John often did. Say what you will about jerks like Al Capone, Cap Streeter, and Big Jim Colosimo (who worked with Hinky Dink and Bathhouse intimately); at least they never made anyone sit through a poem called "Ode to a Bowl of Soup."

O, bowl of soup, to thee I lift my voice in gladsome song
nothing can touch ze spot like what ze French call "booyong."
I like you as mulligatawny, noodles, or consommé.
It cheers me when I see the sign proclaiming "hot soup all day."

It went on like this for several verses. One can only assume that Bathhouse John must have had some real dirt on the reporters who called him "The Bard of the Levee."

In reality, one contemporary, Arthur Sears Henning, said half a century later that Coughlin only ever wrote one poem in his life, "Dear Midnight of Love," which Herbert Asbury described as having "all the literary quality of a first grade essay on 'Oh, see the cat.'" It was put to music and performed by May de Sousa, the daughter of a local cop, at the Chicago Opera House (John asked the city council to adjourn early so they could all go hear it, and May de Sousa went on to be famous in her own right on Broadway). John's song attracted national attention with its inane chorus:

> Dear midnight of love, why did we meet?
> Dear midnight of love, your face is so sweet.
> Pure as the angels above, surely again we shall speak
> Loving only as doves, dear midnight of love.

Bathhouse John sent a copy to every member of the New York Board of Aldermen as Christmas gifts. Alderman Bridges of New York told the *New York Times,* "I could write a better song than that talk of midnight love with my eyes closed." The *Times* suggested that Bridges was jealous, but no one seems to have questioned his odd suggestion that writing songs with one's eyes closed is more challenging than doing it with the eyes open.

This was only the beginning of Coughlin's reputation as a lousy poet. Several other poems appeared under his name with such delightful titles as "She Sleeps at the Side of the Drainage Canal," "They're Tearing Up Clark Street Again," and "Why Did They Make Lake Michigan So Wide?" John Kelley, the police reporter who is said to have been the real author of them, apparently knew perfectly well how dumb they were. Whether Coughlin knew is anyone's guess.

In fact, when talking up a book of his poems in 1909, he told reporters his work "has the red corpuscles. The style is my own. Nobody can counterfeit it." To prove his point, he read a bit from "She Sleeps at the Side of the Drainage Canal."

> In her lonely grave she sleeps tonight
> at the side of the drainage canal;
> Where the whipporwhill calls at the twilight hour
> they planted my sweetheart, Sal
> Just a mile this side of Willow Springs
> not far from the Alton track
> there lieth Sal, my dear old pal
> But these tears won't bring her back.

"Bathhouse John" Coughlin
CHICAGO TRIBUNE

"Is it too deep for you?" he asked. "That's the trouble with a lot of my stuff; it's over the people's heads. Other poets have the same fault." He then told them that if he was in the right frame of mind some day that week, he would compose a sonnet on the subject of plate glass and fire insurance.

No one except Hinky Dink would have had the nerve to tell him how bad they were. The two of them controlled the First Ward—the notorious Levee District, home to bars with names like The Bucket of Blood—for decades, and if Coughlin didn't like you, your life could become very unpleasant.

The *Tribune* once said that Bathhouse was "everything a politician of those days should be: ponderous, yet affable, loud-voiced and stupid." Born in the rough Irish neighborhood known as "Connelly's Patch" in 1860, he was one of the first great Chicago jerks to have been born and raised in the city. At the age of eleven he went to work—one of his earliest jobs was working as a "rubber" in a Turkish bathhouse (which earned him the nickname that stuck with him for life). Mike McDonald, the gambling king of the day, took an interest in the stocky lad and made him an active member, and eventually president, of the First Ward organization. It was good for gamblers like McDonald to put men who would take bribes to give them protection into high places, and Bathhouse John, widely viewed as sort of a good-natured dumbass, was happy to do as he was told.

He did make one smart move, though—early in his political career in 1892, he became acquainted with Mike "Hinky Dink" Kenna, a diminutive saloon owner with a brain in his head who had taken his nickname when he was working as a newsboy. Each ward had two aldermen at the time (aldermen are like the mayors of neighborhoods), and by the middle of the 1890s, Bathhouse and Hinky Dink controlled the First Ward. Coughlin was a large man, Kenna a short one. The two together looked as though they would have made a fine comedy team.

Kenna, the brains of the operation, set up a protection racket that helped the Levee grow into a world famous red-light district. Long-serving Mayor Carter H. Harrison remembered the growing Levee in his autobiography: "From all sides it washed from the ship decks of the Great Lakes, the harvested fields of the far west, the railroad construction works of a dozen states; with this great army came tramps, panhandlers, card sharps, tricksters, mountebanks, circus and sideshow managers, human derelicts of all kinds and descriptions, the weirdest, most fantastic accumulation of beings. The barrelhouse saloons, the ten cent flop lodging houses served as a magnet to draw them together in one squirming mass. Fifty cents a vote became the established rate of exchange." Harrison was first elected with Kenna and Coughlin's support.

Managing this assortment of humanity helped Coughlin and Kenna grow rich and famous. Bathhouse became known far and wide for his fancy green suits and his "poetry." Though he generally did what his backers told him to do in his capacity as a city councilman, he was able to introduce plenty of trivial legislation, like declaring Straw Hat Day, offering rewards to whomever saw the first robin of springtime, and, somewhat ironically, introducing regulations on how women should dress. The silliness of Bathhouse John of the Levee acting as a crusader for public morality was lost on no one.

Together, the two men wielded impressive power in the early twentieth century, and criminals, bookies, and saloon keepers who paid tribute to the two men were able to operate with something approaching immunity. Plenty of people got away with murder because Bathhouse John blocked the investigation. "White slavers," who lured farm girls to the city and then forced them into lives of prostitution, plied their trade under Bathhouse and Hinky Dink's protection. Policemen seldom showed up in the area at all, so thieves and robbers were free to do their jobs unmolested.

All the lowlifes of the district, however, were required to purchase tickets to Bathhouse and Hinky Dink's notorious First Ward Balls, which were held every year, usually at the old Coliseum on Wabash. Descriptions of it today make it seem like an early twentieth-century equivalent of the modern Taste of Chicago, only with madams and saloon keepers previewing their wares instead of restaurants.

Henning called it "an unforgettable spectacle," and the *Tribune* later recalled that the ball "assembled together under one roof the madams and harlots, the robbers and killers, the pickpockets and footpads, the swindlers and thieves, and the drug addicts and common bums who made the levee infamous throughout the world. The latter of these generally came together to frolic and play, to meet the police in jolly good fellowship, to pay their respects to the Bath and the Hink."

Though disguised as a political fundraiser, the ball was generally a bachanalian free-for-all. At midnight, Bathhouse would lead the "grand march" through the hall, resplendently decked out in lavender pants and a suit made of brilliant green billiard cloth decked out in diamond studs, with pink gloves and yellow shoes.

The mayor generally made a show of stopping by for some champagne but made a point of leaving early, before things got rough. The ball, according to Kenna, didn't *really* get exciting until after three in the morning. "Then," reporter Lloyd Wendt wrote, "amid clouds of smoke and the reek of beer, the girls and their cadets, the thugs and plug-uglies, the robbers and sluggers, and the greasy-haired, dress-suited ushers began to fight and play." Booze flowed freely, fights broke out, and sex acts of every description were performed openly.

In Coughlin's seemingly endless attempts to amuse himself, and keep his name in the papers, in 1912 he issued a list of the ten handsomest men in the city. Hinky Dink was notably absent. "Hinky Dink's handsome, but he's kind of skinny," Coughlin explained. Instead, he gave nods to state's attorney John E. W. Wayman ("intensely masculine"), former alderman Milton Forman ("exceptionally handsome forehead"), and attorney Hamilton Lewis ("general style—gothic").

Mayor Carter H. Harrison topped the list, and Bathhouse noted that the mayor "probably would be elected president, if the women could vote."

Votes for women were coming in faster than Coughlin guessed. The next June, the Illinois Legislature passed the Municipal Voting Act, giving Illinois women the right to vote several years before the United States Constitution extended the right to other American women. Before the governor even had time to sign the act, the new voters of Chicago announced that they were "going after" Hinky Dink and Bathhouse John. Their first order of business, one organization said, would be getting the Levee District closed down.

Fights were put up, and Coughlin was accused of any number of evils, but he managed to survive every wave of reform, even as the Levee District shrank around him, the First Ward balls were canceled, and the Capone gang gradually took over "real" control of the Levee.

Though now lacking his old political power, Bathhouse kept his seat on the city council and continued to be active in public life, and, using the wealth he'd already built up, bought a zoo in Colorado and a full stable of sixty race horses (remarkably, he almost never won at the races, even when he owned most of the horses). He would spend most of his time holding court at the Silver Dollar Saloon on Madison Street and insisted on keeping the annual Straw Hat Day alive, even though newspapers proclaiming Straw Hat Day a flop became an annual event in the 1930s. Papers showed him gleefully practicing putting on his straw pith helmet.

He was still the alderman of the First Ward upon his death in 1938. The whole town came out for his funeral, including the Mayor and Hinky Dink, who had retired from public life.

In 2011, a theater troupe called This Is Not the Studio put on a tribute to the First Ward Ball, featuring a performance of "Dear Midnight of Love," Bathhouse John's greatest hit. It was probably the first time the song had been performed in years.

One can only hope.

CHAPTER 14

William J. Davis
Corner-Cutting Killer

The history of Chicago is littered with men who cut corners, ignored rules, bribed officials, and broke the law to make an extra few bucks.

Sometimes it accomplishes little besides making them look like jerks. Take, for instance, Rod Blagojevich, who lost his job as governor, not to mention his own liberty, when he tried to sell the Senate seat that became vacant when Senator Obama was elected president. The FBI released several tapes of him swearing like a sailor as he tried to take advantage of the "golden" opportunity that had fallen into his lap to appoint someone to the Senate, which he wasn't about to let go for nothing.

It was a terrible thing to do and huge embarrassment for the State of Illinois, as well as making him look even LESS popular in a state where his percentage approval rating had already fallen into the twenties.

But no one *died* because of what he did.

And sometimes that's what happens when you ignore regulations, take bribes, and cut corners. Sometimes a *lot* of people die.

That's what happened when William J. Davis, a theater manager, cut corner after corner in building and managing the Iroquois Theatre. Built in 1903, the Iroquois was to be the crown jewel of Chicago's new theater district in The Loop—the rival of any theater in New York or Paris. And it was, by all accounts, gorgeous.

But, though it was advertised as "absolutely fireproof" in playbills (which really just seems like it was begging to tempt fate), a massive fire ravaged the building during a matinee barely a month after the theater was first opened to the public.

The exact body count for the tragedy is in dispute, but most estimates hover around six hundred—roughly twice as many as

A breathtaking panorama of the auditorium taken shortly after the fire
LIBRARY OF CONGRESS

died in the Great Chicago Fire. An early account spoke of the "sudden transformation of a playhouse filled with a pleasure-seeking throng into an inferno filled with the shrieking living and mutilated dead." A doctor on the scene, who had been on duty during the Great Fire and served in the Army of the Potomac during the Civil War, said he had never seen anything to equal the carnage.

There were lots of jerks involved here—the building commissioner was grossly negligent, the building inspector was equally bad (both had presumably been bribed), the fire marshal failed miserably at enforcing the fire codes, and the mayor should probably have been held responsible for having such goons in his employ in the first place. Even most of the stagehands, carpenters, and technicians should have been more vocal in bringing the theater's deficiencies to light. And this is to say nothing of the grave robbers who poured into the theater when it was still smoldering to plunder the bodies, yanking necklaces from necks, shimmying rings from fingers and jerking earrings off of ears (an urban legend at the time said that one man had his hand cut off by vigilantes after being caught cutting off a woman's fingers to get her rings—papers *did* report that a hand was found in the rubble some time later).

But for the purposes of this book, we'll be picking on one particular jerk: William J. Davis, the theater's general manager. He's hardly the only man who can be said to have blood on his hands, but if any man was responsible for the way the theater was built and managed, it was him.

Will Davis began his life with a promising enough start—he had volunteered for the Union Navy at the age of fourteen during the Civil War, but slid downhill from there, taking a job after the war with the IRS before moving to Chicago and falling into the theatrical profession.

By the turn of the twentieth century, he had managed enough theaters to know the ins and outs of the business, and to know everyone he might have to bribe to get a theater opened quickly, despite all the cut corners that plagued many of them (that most of the theaters in town were "death traps" was well known). In 1901, he teamed up with Harry Powers as joint owner and manager of the Iroquois Theatre, a new theater that the two planned to build. Davis was determined to give theater-goers the best possible experience—he wanted the new theater to be a "temple of the drama."

And, by all appearances, it was. The architect, twenty-eight-year-old wunderkind George Marshall, did a fantastic job. But Davis seems to have failed to take into account the fact that most people enjoy the theater a whole lot more when they *aren't* being trampled or burned to death.

After considerable delays, ground for the new theater was broken on Randolph Street, between State and Dearborn (right on the site of the saloon where George Trussell was killed, and across the street from the old *Chicago Times* office), in July of 1903. It was open and ready for business by the end of November, after barely three months of work. Chicagoans accustomed to seeing construction companies spend years just trying to fill a pothole can probably imagine that corners must have been cut to get a building erected so quickly.

And cut they were. Since a sprinkler system would have been costly, and unsightly, none was ever installed. Hallways were not nearly as wide as they were required to be by law. And though laws had mandated that all theaters in the city had doors opening outward, toward the street, to ease evacuation, the doors at the Iroquois opened inward, toward the lobby. Every theater was required to have a fireproof asbestos curtain to contain fires that broke out on stage, and the Iroquois had one, but they had saved fifty-six dollars by using a blend of asbestos, cotton, and wood pulp. It was about as fireproof as a box of matches.

And, lest anyone think that this "temple of drama" would be devoted to high-brow entertainment, the first show that ran there was a Christmas panto called *Mr. Bluebeard,* which featured such immortal songs as "Come and Buy Our Luscious Fruits," "Oriental Slaves Are We," and "A Most Unpopular Potentate"—none of which had much to do with the plot, which, to the extent that the show had one at all, concerned a guy who kills his wives and hangs them up on meat hooks, but also included a bizarre sequence where Sister Anne (played by Eddie Foy, the star of the show) turns into Shakespeare's Ophelia in a fit of dementia and sings a tune called "Hamlet Was a Melancholy Dane."

But as dumb as the show was, the songs were catchy and the sheer spectacle of it was top-notch. There was an aerial ballet, a cast of around three hundred, and plenty of great dancing. For the matinee on December 30, about two thousand tickets were sold (a couple of hundred more than they could comfortably seat). Midway through the second act, the orchestra stopped playing when a calcium light offstage arced and hurled a couple of carbon sparks into the muslin drapes that hung on the walls. A stage hand tried to put it out, but to no avail. The flames kept climbing toward the ceiling.

Eddie Foy stepped onstage and pleaded for people to remain calm, assuming that the fire would soon burn itself out (it was apparently not the first time the drape had caught fire). But this time, the fire began to catch on the scenery that was hanging in the rafters—much of which had been painted with oil-based paint.

The fire curtain, useless though it was, didn't even lower all the way—it got caught on a lighting rig partway down.

And no one realized that management had shut off all the ventilation to the building, so that when the backstage door was opened for the actors to escape, a backdraft created a "balloon of fire" that blew off the stage and into the auditorium.

Naturally, everyone panicked and ran. Eddie Foy continued to plead for calm (and stayed on stage far longer than it was safe for him to do so), but his pleas didn't mean much to people who had just seen a fireball shoot offstage.

And the cut corners led to a few problems as the patrons tried to evacuate.

For one thing, in order to cut down on the number of poor people who might sneak in, the fire exits were kept locked. In a calm situation, patrons could probably have figured out how to operate the fancy "French" locking system on the doors, but the panicking crowd was useless when it came to that sort of problem-solving, and anyone who tried to work the door wound up being crushed against it.

When they couldn't get out of a fire exit, several began a stampede toward the main exits onto Randolph, expecting to push through the doors and out to safety.

But here there were two problems: One was that the doors opened in, toward the lobby; another was that they were locked, as well. No one crashed through the doors—they just crashed *into* the doors. And then into each other. Some were trampled beyond all recognition.

Things were no better on the balcony. Only one hallway led to the lower level, and *that* had been blocked off by a metal accordion gate to keep people from sneaking into the better seats. Even if they'd reached the door beyond it, they'd have found it locked.

After fifteen minutes, when the fire had burned itself out, piles of bodies choked every exit. Another pile sat in the alley back behind the theater, where people had been pushed out of a balcony fire exit that wasn't connected to a completed fire escape yet.

For days, the newspapers carried gruesome accounts, not just of the fire, but of the terrible stories of mothers looking for their lost children. One woman was so horrified by the stories that she sort of snapped—after reading the paper, she threw her children

The stage after the fire
LIBRARY OF CONGRESS

under the bed and started chopping her wood stove to bits with an axe before it could start a fire in her home.

Other readers wrote to the paper to note flaws they'd noticed at the Iroquois when they were there themselves. One man pointed out that there had been no aisles at all between the seats and the boxes. He had been seated next to a box at a recent performance, and it had taken him thirty minutes to get out of the theater after the show.

After the fire, Davis and Powers set up camp in one of the women's dressing rooms, from which they issued a statement that they had given up more space in the building to exits and aisles than any other theater in the country. No one exactly believed them. And on January 1, the day after the fire, a warrant for Davis's arrest for manslaughter was sworn out by one Arthur Hull, whose wife, three children, and maid had all been killed.

Actually, dozens of employees, officials, and actors were arrested and called in for an inquest. But the police chief made it very clear to the press that he did not hold most of the actors responsible—they were simply needed as witnesses, and were victims, not criminals. "These girls are not responsible for the casualty in any way," said Chief O'Neill. He didn't say the same of Will Davis or Harry Powers.

The coroner's jury found all sorts of problems when they investigated the theater. City laws regarding fire alarm boxes had been ignored. Regulations about the fireproofing of scenery and woodwork were not followed. The asbestos curtain was clearly inadequate; only traces could be found at all. There weren't nearly enough exits on the balcony. Signs designating what exits there were had never been posted. The top balcony was too steep. There was only one reel of fire hose in the house.

When it came time to name the responsible parties, the coroner's jury named Will J. Davis first and foremost.

For his part, Davis could only fall back on a classic excuse: It wasn't his fault—he was just too incompetent to see how badly things had been set up. "I trusted everything to my employees and supposed that the theater was fully equipped and the safest in the world," he said. "I had given orders to have the best of everything."

If he'd given the orders, though, he apparently never did a thing to make sure they were being followed. Countless men and women before or since have been in the same situation: not taking a security measure or two that they should have because they never thought it would be an issue. Most of us have probably been guilty of this once or twice in our lives. Practically every theater owner in town was just as guilty as he was.

But Davis ended up on trial for manslaughter.

The build-up to the trial was delayed for some time, and Davis complained a bit that his reputation had suffered. "The public," he said, "has been unjust to me. It would be just as fair to hold the president of a railroad company for manslaughter because there was an explosion in one of the railroad trains, and fire ensued, and passengers were burned to death. . . . why should we be charged with murder because an audience stampeded?"

It would have been a fair enough question, if the building had truly been up to code. But it wasn't. Davis had cut corners everywhere, from the building of the theater to his rush to open for business without bothering to train the ushers as to what to do in an emergency. To assume that a crowd would react calmly in the event of a fire was simply foolish.

Knowing that he'd never be acquitted in Chicago, Davis successfully managed to have the trial moved out to Danville, where the case dragged on for more than three years. Finally, on March 9, 1907, Davis was freed on a technicality—the real cause is buried under legalese, but the gist of it is that the fire provisions ordered by the city were not legally enforceable laws; they were more "suggestions" than anything else, from a legal standpoint. The judge ruled that while Davis was "morally guilty," he could not be found "legally guilty." He stated, "if it were in my power to bring back those young girls to life by putting the defendant in this case in the penitentiary for the rest of his natural life I believe I could do it, but I cannot . . . I am inclined to overrule the defendant's motion, but again I cannot." He noted that the shame Davis would endure was far worse than life in prison or the death penalty could ever have been.

Since Davis was found not guilty, the same ruling applied to the others who were standing trial. No one was ever held accountable for the six hundred-odd deaths that the poorly built and poorly managed theater had brought about.

And Davis, though he was certainly haunted by the events, doesn't seem to have lived the life of shame that the judge imagined for him. He continued in the theater world for a few more years before retiring, and died in 1919 at the age of seventy-five.

But those close to him said that he never quite recovered from the trauma, and a century later he ended up in a book about dead jerks.

CHAPTER 15

Johann Hoch
An Affinity for Arsenic

I am the kind of guy who has a favorite serial killer. And mine is Johann Hoch, one of the biggest goofballs ever to stand trial after killing a dozen or so women. When the police caught up with Hoch in New York, he had already proposed to what police estimated would be his fifty-fifth wife—and possibly his fifteenth or sixteenth murder victim.

One would think a guy who convinced that many women to marry him must have been a pretty suave individual, but he wasn't an attractive man—he was a stout, wheezy sort of guy who might be considered a good catch if you were the sort of person whose ideal man is the guy on the Pringles can.

He spoke like a German-dialect comedian as the police accompanied him back to Chicago, where he was suspected of murdering one of his recent wives, Marie, then robbing and deserting her sister Amelia (to whom he'd proposed while Marie's coffin was still in the room), to stand trial.

Reporters and police tried to needle him into a confession just to pass the time as the train rolled through the prairie.

"Come on, Hoch," they said. "How come you married so many women?"

Hoch laughed. Newspapers tried to transcribe his accent as he gave his reply: "Oh, all der vimmen for Johann go crazy, ja?"

"All right," they said. "How come so many of them are dead now?"

He laughed again. "Kidney failure, I suppose," he quipped.

And he wasn't far off. Many of them *had* died of kidney failure. He was just declining to add the fact that the kidney failure was the result of nephritis, the disease they'd contracted when he gave them arsenic powder with their food at the post-wedding feast.

A FEW OF HOCH'S NUMEROUS ALLEGED WIVES.

Wives of Johann Hoch
NEW YORK WORLD

When Hoch began his career as a "bluebeard," a sort of killer who marries and kills a series of spouses for their money, murder by arsenic was still a perfect crime. Arsenic was an ingredient in embalming fluid, so the moment an undertaker stepped into a room with the corpse, it was impossible to get a conviction. It wasn't as clean a kill as just shooting or stabbing someone, though—arsenic poisoning killed its victims only after days of agony as their bladder and kidneys were ravaged.

Hoch was a goofy guy that the police couldn't help but like, but he was as cold-blooded a killer as has ever existed.

A Chicago American *illustration of Hoch using his hypnotic powers on women. It seemed far-fetched, but no more so than thinking a man such as Hoch could charm so many women into marrying him by any normal means.*
CHICAGO DAILY AMERICAN

Johann Hoch seems to have come to the United States in the middle of the 1890s. According to several witnesses, he worked as an apprentice or janitor in a building at 63rd Street, the infamous Murder Castle, where his boss had been none other than H. H. Holmes. Whether he was actually an employee of Holmes remains an open mystery, though by most accounts he came to the United States too late to have met him. It's hard to be sure; most serial killers of the day were adept at covering their tracks by fudging the records, and Holmes made reference to a man who sure sounded like Hoch in one of his confessions.

Unlike Holmes, who was always trying new ways to kill people and make a bunch of cash from the murder, Hoch established one standard modus operandi: he would meet a frumpy, middle-aged widow or spinster, woo her, marry her, take her money, and run off with it. Usually, this would all be done in the course of less than a week. Murder was only necessary about a third of the time.

It was a method that worked for him; he knew just what to say to a middle-aged spinster. He was a fat, wheezy little fellow who had learned to spot a sort of woman who could be seduced by mere sweet talk (though throwing in promises of a life of ease to women who were resigned to lives of hard work didn't hurt). He once said that nine out of ten women could be won by flattery.

How many times he repeated this routine is unknown, but it's likely to be high—as with Holmes, estimates range from the dozens to the hundreds. He went to jail for a while early in his career and probably even faked his death at one point, emerging with a new name (taken from his ex-wife) and plans to start all over.

It was the last couple of adventures in Chicago that really got him in trouble.

Born to the name Jacob Schmidt, Johann Hoch is merely his best-known alias. The name "Hoch" was taken from his first Chicago wife, Caroline Hoch, whom he married shortly after arriving in the city. As with most of his marriages, it was a short one. Only days after the wedding, the minister who had performed the ceremony came to call on Caroline and found her writhing in agony in her bed. He remembered seeing her husband, then known as Jacob Huff, giving her some white powder after the wedding, but he had thought it was simply medicine. When Caroline died, she was quickly buried, and Jacob disappeared, leaving his clothes by the river and hoping that everyone would think he had drowned.

Some years later in 1900, when Hoch was brought into police custody after screwing up a job selling furniture that didn't belong to him (an H. H. Holmes trick if there ever was one), the minister recognized him and alerted police that Hoch might have been up to a lot more than just a routine furniture swindle. They exhumed Caroline Hoch's body and found that several internal organs were mysteriously missing. Hoch was arrested for murder, but there was no real evidence to convict him, and he was eventually released.

For the next four years, Hoch went on a spree in Chicago, marrying several other women and killing them when it seemed convenient and simply ditching them when it didn't.

The last to be murdered was one Marie Walcker, a widow in her forties who owned a candy store at Willow and Larabee. She had answered an ad in a German newspaper in which Hoch described himself as a "widower, 43 years old, worth $8000," in search of a wife, up to the age of forty-five, who would "make home pleasant." Marie Walcker was forty-six, but Hoch received a letter from her on December 3, and on December 5 he came to inspect the candy shop. They drank coffee in the back with one of Mrs. Walcker's friends, and Mr. Hoch popped the question:

"Do you like me?" he asked.

"Yes, if you like me," she replied.

"Well," he said, "you like me, and I like you, so we can get married, yes?"

This was, in essence, a business proposal more than a romantic one. Hoch would later insist that all of his marriages were simply for money. "I never loved any of my wives," he said. "I had no use for women."

On December 6, Mrs. Walcker sold the candy store for $75 on Hoch's orders, then withdrew an additional sum of $195 from the bank. The two were married in the court house on December 10, and the next morning Hoch took the $270 from Marie's purse to put into his bank account, and the two moved into his cottage near 63rd and Union, only a short jaunt from the infamous H. H. Holmes's Murder Castle.

The marriage was a long one, as Hoch's marriages went. Maria didn't become ill until December 17, more than a week after the marriage began, and she lingered with the disease for more than three weeks, lying her bed as the arsenic-induced nephritis wreaked havoc her lower abdominal region. She complained that she couldn't control her bladder, but she suffered severe pain in urinating and was described as "pale and yellow and vomiting frequently." Her pains and their treatments would later be described in gruesome detail during Hoch's trial; just shooting her and melting the body down would have been far more humane.

And while she lay there, slowly and painfully peeing herself to death, Hoch made a great show of sympathy for *himself.*

His first wife had been sick for eighteen years, he told visitors, and he thought he had finally got a healthy woman and was terribly disappointed. It's hard to imagine anyone feeling for *him* while Marie was in agony, subject to frequent enemas and catheters, unable to eat anything without puking it back up, but Hoch's attitude was so ingratiating that people actually tried to comfort *him* as he threw himself a pity party.

Though Hoch kissed Marie every morning and insisted that she be cared for, whatever the expense, he didn't attend to her much himself. Most of the necessary care was given to her by her sister, Amelie Fischer, on whom Johann doted. Even in her weakened state, Marie began to get jealous of her sister, and all the attention her own new husband was giving her.

On January 11, Marie called her sister to her bed—now her death bed—and said, in a bitter tone, "Take him . . . you human sow."

As she finally passed on, Hoch launched into another pity party for himself. "Now I am a widower again," he wailed. "All alone in the world!"

As Marie's body was taken downstairs to be prepared for burial, Hoch proposed marriage to her sister. Amelie said it was not time to talk about such things yet, but Hoch said it made no difference. "The dead belong to the dead," he said, "and the living to the living. . . . if Marie had not insulted you I would have mourned six weeks for her, but under the circumstances we must marry right away."

He immediately began to woo her by making plans to bring the ten children she had left in Germany over to the United States. He would rent out his current house and build a three-story brick home on the corner for her children. They could open a hotel and run it together. They could take a honeymoon trip to Germany.

By the end of the day, Mrs. Fischer had accepted the proposal. Marie was buried on January 16, and her widower married her sister two days later.

But several of Marie's friends already believed that she had been poisoned. When the newlyweds came home to Amelie's house, one of her friends was waiting in the parlor. As soon as Amelie's back was turned, Hoch fled—having already taken $750 from her bank account.

Two days later, while the police searched for Hoch, Marie's body was exhumed. Arsenic was found in the stomach, and more was found in other organs when the body was exhumed a second time a few months later. In previous years, this would have been a perfect crime—but not anymore. The body had been embalmed with letheform, a new kind of fluid that contained no arsenic. This was Hoch's fatal mistake—he hadn't been keeping abreast of changes in the undertaking industry.

Hoch was found in a rooming house in New York, where he had already proposed to the proprietress. Officers who arrested him found that his fountain pen was filled with arsenic.

"That's tooth powder," Holmes said.

"Tooth powder, hell!" the officer cried. "When it's analyzed we'll find it's arsenic. A man doesn't carry tooth powder in the barrel of a fountain pen."

Eventually, Hoch would change his story slightly and claim that the substance was "headache powder." Later he admitted that it was poison, all right, but said that he had been planning to use it on himself.

But he sure seemed to be in a jovial mood for a guy who was carrying around poison with which to commit suicide. By this time, the papers had been following his story for some time, and Hoch was taken back to Chicago as something of a celebrity. He joked with the guards all the way.

Woman after woman came forward with tales of being swindled by him, and police inspector George Shippy estimated that he may have killed as many as forty women in his long career. New, strange rumors spread as fast as William Randolph Hearst's *Chicago American* could make them up. Soon, people were whispering not only that Hoch was a pupil of H. H. Holmes, but also that he was the twin brother of Louis Thombs, a murderer who had been hanged a few years before, and that he had hypnotized women into marrying him using some sort of magic zither. The *American* had come into being too late to have any fun with the furor over Holmes that other papers had enjoyed a few years before, and now was their chance to replay the whole sordid affair, as they raced to find a way to connect Holmes to Hoch with something more concrete than simply establishing that he had once had his hair cut in a barbershop on the first floor of the old Murder Castle on 63rd. Plenty of Castle residents swore they had known him; others insisted they hadn't. As with anything else to do with Holmes, it's hard to tell whom to believe. The guards warned Hoch that dozens of women were waiting to meet him in Chicago, all claiming to be his ex-wives. He laughed until tears rolled down his face. But even if most of them were lying, as Hoch insisted, it was quite apparent that he had spent much of the previous ten years going from town to town, plying his trade as a professional marriage artist.

"I suppose," he said, "that I've got to suffer for every man that ever deserted a woman and could not be found afterward. Come on, ladies, if any of you have lost husbands . . . just step around and identify me! Why, I see now [in the papers] that an unidentified Iroquois Theater fire body was one of my wives. Ha! Ha! Oh, this is rich!"

All along the train, he kept entertaining the press and the guards, as they tried to trip him up into admitting that he'd been married several times.

"What about Mrs. Hedrickson?" they asked. "She identified you this morning."

"Oh, her eyesight was always poor!" Hoch said with a hearty laugh.

"How do you know, if she was never your wife?" asked the reporter.

"Ah, that's the joke!" he cried. "That's the joke! Don't ask me to explain it now—wait til I get to Chicago, and then we'll all enjoy the joke—the police and all."

According to the news reports, he had to hold onto nearby bars to keep from falling to the floor with laughter. When asked the names of the women he'd married, he simply said they were all named "Mrs. Johann Hoch" and laughed again.

The press was fascinated, writing that "the little fat man, with a red, round face and a semi-bald, hair-fringed head seems to have regarded the world of gullible femininity as his special preserve, to be hunted at pleasure. He was a connoisseur of German widows."

Hoch continued to treat his whole arrest as a joke for weeks, and went back and forth between denying that he'd married so many women and bragging about it. "Flattery was my chief stock in trade," he explained to a reporter from the *New York Times*. "You can win a woman quicker that way than any other."

While in the county jail, Hoch lived very well for a prisoner. He had a fine couch in his cell and lived on porterhouse steaks and beer, instead of bread and water, like most prisoners (police said that this was to get him to confess, but most assumed that bribery was involved). He was even allowed to go on walks outside of the prison, during which he demonstrated his prowess as a Don Juan by flirting with every passing woman.

No matter how gruesome the stories about him got, or how gruesome he was as a person, the ladies loved him. He received dozens of valentines and marriage proposals (from very strange women, one can assume) while he was in jail. Women claiming to be his ex-wives gathered at the police station—frumpy middle-aged women, for the most part. Many were not there to accuse him—they simply wanted him back.

Oddest of all, perhaps, was that Hoch's greatest ally as his trial began was none other than Amelie Fischer Hoch, his last Chicago wife, who came to his cell daily to dote on him, bring him presents, darn his socks, and beg forgiveness. He barely acknowledged her, but she didn't seem hurt when Hoch supported efforts to frame her for her sister's murder.

Meanwhile, of course, Hoch still confidently believed that he had committed only the perfect crime of arsenic poisoning. It was only when the undertaker took the stand and testified that the embalming fluid he'd used contained no arsenic that Hoch began to appear frightened. His demeanor changed visibly after he realized his mistake.

Even with a clear guilty verdict for his role in the death of Marie Walcker Hoch, appeals dragged on and on and Hoch continued to use his considerable charms to raise more money. He even got the endorsement of a group of spiritualists who had been told he was innocent by his dead wives on "the other side," but none of these were sufficient to overturn the verdict, and he was hanged in the county jail in 1906—against the objections of some of the jailers, who had grown to like the little fiend.

Years later, the county physician remembered the scene when Mrs. Amelie Fischer Hoch came to the jail to collect her now-late husband's effects. "She drove away," he said, "with a suitcase full of souvenirs of the man who had poisoned her sister, proposed to herself within sight of his wife's coffin, made her a bigamous bridge, and absconded with her laboriously earned savings. She had denounced him, she had brought him to a death sentence, she had forgiven him, and comforted his captivity, and now she was preparing to weep over the worthless articles he had left behind. You can learn about women from her."

Some say the county physician was a bit of a jerk, too.

CHAPTER 16

David D. Healy
Dereliction and Death at Dunning

Here's one to think over: Just how corrupt, how abusive, and how big a jerk did you have to be to be censured for your conduct as president of an insane asylum in the nineteenth century?

In the 1800s, mental health was not as well understood as it is now, and stories about abuses at mental hospitals—which were then given cheery names like "lunatic asylum"—were rampant. If there's an abandoned insane asylum in your town, odds are very good that people tell horror stories about what used to go on in there.

The stories may or may not be accurate, but what *really* went on in there was probably even worse. People in those days would drop insane relatives off at the asylum and just leave them there. Often, they'd tell people that they'd died. And when they *really* died, they'd often simply be buried in an unmarked grave on the asylum grounds. If, again, you have an abandoned mental hospital in your town, odds are good that there are lots and lots of dead bodies buried on the grounds. In some small towns, unmarked graves at the mental hospital outnumber living citizens by a comfortable margin.

In the late nineteenth century, Chicago's premier mental hospital was a place called the Cook County Insane Asylum at Dunning—simply "Dunning" for short—and was situated on the Far Northwest Side, not far from the intersection of Harlem and Irving Park. When construction of luxury homes in a nearby area was started in the late 1980s, lots and lots of graves were found— mass graves, simple graves . . . even one guy who was so well preserved that they could still see his mutton chops and handlebar mustache. Though Dunning Cemetery covered some eighty acres, people had simply forgotten that it was ever there.

Records were not always well kept, but in years from which there were records, it seemed that the cemetery averaged five hun-

An infirmary room at Dunning after a fire
CHICAGO DAILY NEWS

dred to one thousand burials annually. It was conservatively estimated that the grounds, some of which were by then underneath a parking lot and strip mall, were providing a resting place for at least thirty-eight thousand bodies, including more than a hundred victims of the Great Chicago Fire, the unclaimed bodies of the poor and friendless (including that of serial killer Johann Hoch), and the bodies of the inmates of the insane asylum at Dunning.

The discovery of so many graves was a chilling reminder of just how we treated the mentally ill in those days.

To the city's credit, there was usually an outcry when horror stories came out—such as the time in 1913 when a patient was found beaten to death by attendants, or when patients died of scurvy or starvation, but these are just the events that made the papers. It's quite likely that most of the worst abuses went unrecorded. Rumors that doctors who wanted bodies for dissection and experiments could select live patients from the "killing ward" and have their remains in a trunk the next day were never quite confirmed (and were obviously denied vehemently by authorities), but there were witnesses who swore it was true.

The mental hospital at Dunning was founded in 1851, at a time when it was still a prairie there—a good place for a combination insane asylum and "poor farm" where the poor could be given a place to work. The two institutions were kept in the same building—described as little better than collections of filthy prison cells—for several years, until a new building was finally built to house the insane asylum. By the 1880s, new additions allowed it to accommodate as many as one thousand patients at once, and it had its own train line to bring supplies. Some say that this train line was the origin of the phrase "crazy train."

Various investigations found all sorts of scandals, including bribery, cover-ups, nepotism, and gambling rings being held inside of the asylum. The entire management was censured following an investigation in 1895.

It's difficult to pinpoint just one single jerk who stands out among the others. Healy, the president of the county board who was responsible for the place, is probably as good a point to fix the blame as any. Superintendent Morgan, though, was more directly involved.

In 1895, Dunning attendants murdered George Pucik, an iron-molder who had gone insane and was boarding in Ward D W 2 of the asylum. He had just arrived there that week after being shuffled around through various other hospitals, each of which found him to be in pretty good shape, physically.

The morning after he arrived, he was taken to be washed by a pair of attendants. When he became "unruly," the two attendants responded by beating and kicking him.

The attendants said that it was all a case of self-defense, and one of them had the bruises to prove it—he said that Pucik had hit him.

"What did you do when the patient struck you?" he was asked.

"Why, I became angry and went back at him," he replied.

"Do you mean that you beat him and kicked him?"

"No, not exactly. I only showed him that I was in charge of the ward he was in."

Clearly, he had done more. Pucik's breast bone was broken, some ribs were fractured, and that evening he died from shock and hemorrhage caused by the injuries.

The other attendant issued a confession. They had found Pucik hiding under his bed, and had kicked the heck out of him, starting with a kick to the chest that led him to "halloo" and slump to the ground, unconscious. The two attendants had dragged the limp body to a basin to wash him. He never regained consciousness.

When the story broke, people began to call for an investigation into conditions at Dunning, though Healy, the president of the county board, resisted all such efforts mightily, insisting that public investigations were a waste of time. He was quite casual when faced with accusations that bad things were going on in the asylum. "I think," he said, when asked, "that possibly there may be some truth in [that]. Doubtless much evil is smothered before it has a chance to reach the ears of those in authority." Healy, for his part, had enacted a civil service plan that was supposed to eliminate patronage, but was said, in practice, to simply put his own "henchmen" into high places.

The fact that he, and everyone else in a position of authority, was so against a probe only made people more suspicious. Horror stories about Dunning had been going on for some time already; the previous December, in 1894, an affidavit describing cruelties taking place there filed by an attendant named Riddle led to a brief investigation that showed that other attendants were in the habit of roaming around with billy clubs and gas pipes that they used to beat patients. The attendants were often drunk and negligent, and management didn't seem to care much. But at the time, the board was so caught up dealing with patronage debates that they hadn't bothered to do much about it.

The problems certainly continued. One employee estimated that there were about sixty deaths a month at Dunning, between the poorhouse and the insane asylum, of which he knew of at least four that should have led to investigations, but none were made. One of the employees, the undertaker said, had tried but failed to get an investigation going. "[That employee] did most of the kicking about the way things were run while I was there," he said. "He was soon discharged, and that taught the other kickers a lesson."

The way the dead were treated wasn't much better. While he didn't say anything about a killing ward, the undertaker said, "If the people of Cook County knew how human bodies are treated out at that morgue they would go out there and tear the whole place down. The morgue is a shame and a disgrace to the county. Bodies are frequently stacked up there like dead animals . . . and buried like so many hogs. . . . with their clothes on, the trousers and shirts in which they died, and a piece of cotton or horsehair under the head."

The living inmates, he said, were packed like cattle and had little or no heat in the winter. No attempt at all was made at sanitation, and "the air is foul, reeking with the stench arising from filthy clothing and filthier bodies of the unfortunate hundreds who are huddled in there to escape death from freezing and starving outside . . . but any employee who dares to open his mouth in protest might as well look for another job. Mum is the word from the superintendent down to the lowest scrubwoman about the premises."

When the story hit the press, an investigation was called, and more and more stories began to come out. It quickly became clear that Superintendent Morgan had no idea what was going on in the place.

But by the time the investigation really got underway, the attendants had had plenty of time to clean things up and give them a veneer of respectability.

Jane Addams, the noted social reformer of Hull House, was on the committee of investigators. She had only been running Hull House for a few years but was already one of the most famous and respected women in the city. "It is very plain to be seen," she said, "that the whole institution is on dress parade . . .

I have visited Dunning off and on for years and never did I see things so nearly perfect."

Still, plenty of trouble was found and Healy went on one rant after another, insisting that the investigation was a waste of time and berating the investigators while accusing others of taking bribes. His only evidence of bribery was the word of the asylum's butcher, Miles W. Evans, who was found to be "not worthy of belief."

There were two reports issued—a majority report that was fairly unfavorable, and a minority report that made Healy look better. Healy used his influence to get the minority report adopted. An effort to indict Healy was still considered, but it never really went anywhere. He still had his job a couple of years later, when more scandals broke out when it became known that bodies were being stolen from the morgue.

In 1912, the state bought Dunning from the county for one dollar and took over the operations, but conditions were still slow to improve. And whoever was in charge of records did a lousy job; though record keepers were meticulous about recording exactly how much was being paid for coffin nails, they didn't do much to keep records of where the coffins were actually being buried. The land where the bodies were buried was sold to developers who shrugged their shoulders and built right over it.

CHAPTER 17

Harry Spencer
A Killer Imagination

No one was ever held responsible for the six hundred or so deaths in the Iroquois Theatre disaster of 1903. A few guys were convicted of crimes related to it, though—two months after the disaster, three men were convicted of stealing two hundred bucks and a watch off of a corpse.

And one of the other "ghouls" may have been hanged a decade later.

According to Henry Spencer's story, told to reporters as he sat in his cell, awaiting execution for murder, he was helping to carry dead bodies to a morgue when he noticed a "richly gowned" woman who was burned beyond recognition but was wearing some awfully nice jewelry. That night, he took a female friend to identify the body. The friend told authorities that the body was her sister, Nellie Skarupa, and took possession of the remains.

"We got $1,500 for the jewelry besides $500 in cash off her," he boasted. "I guess she's still buried under that name."

But the records didn't match Henry's story. Indeed, he may be one of the few murderers in Chicago history who actually was quite a bit less of a jerk than he thought he was himself.

At this time, Harry Spencer was thirty-two years old and looked like the kind of mild-mannered young man who might work as an accounting clerk. The *Chicago Examiner* said he looked like a seminary student in his wire-rim glasses.

But when he was arrested for murdering a woman with a pistol and hammer, he bragged that he had murdered twenty-eight women and claimed that he was "the greatest criminal of the century." He wasn't clear on names or dates, but could tell whether he "beat 'em to death with a hammer," or "shot 'em to death," without hesitation when recounting his crimes.

He confessed to a handful of unsolved murders. "I am sore on the world and I don't care," he said. "Nobody's life has meant much to me. My own life doesn't amount to much to me. I know I'll swing for this and I figure it will take about two months more to get over the bickering about it. I wouldn't care if they pulled it off in the morning and had it over with."

They showed him a picture of two of the girls he claimed to have killed and asked how he'd done it.

"Oh, I just beat their heads in and threw them in the lake."

"What was next?"

"I took a woman over to the Northwest side, killed her, and burned her up."

On and on he spoke, of beating women with a hammer, robbing candy stores, pushing men down elevator shafts, robbing cash registers, holding up restaurants, killing people, and breaking things— everything but stealing candy from children. He spoke of his boyhood in Chicago orphanages in the Levee District, his teenage years in the prison, and his favorite pastime: swindling women. He even spoke of marrying one woman, then walking her twelve miles into the woods to show her some land that he claimed to own, where he brained her with a hammer. He had tried to go straight when he first got out of jail, but washing dishes for sixteen hours a day at five dollars a week in a Clark Street restaurant had left him bitter and "sore at the world."

"If Spencer is the arch murderer that he confesses to be," said police captain Halpin, "he stands alone in the criminal history of the western world."

But he wasn't all that he claimed.

Over the course of his long confession, his tales got taller and taller. He spoke of having stolen 182 bicycles and pawned them. Of having held up practically every place on Clark. Of having killed numerous women with the same three-pound hammer. Of smoking "hop," chewing tobacco, and of sometimes smoking fifteen or twenty "pills" in half an hour. Of stealing lots and lots of jewelry, none of which was ever pawned, because he didn't trust the pawnbrokers, who he said were all Jewish.

Spencer looked like a seminary
student in his glasses . . .
CHICAGO DAILY EXAMINER

. . . but more like a regular hoodlum when he posed without them in
his cell.
CHICAGO DAILY EXAMINER

"Of course I kill women," he said at one point. "That's what makes me a classier prisoner than these cheap robbers."

The stories, however, didn't hold up to any fact checking. Some of the unsolved crimes he'd confessed to were committed while he was locked up in prison. Other stories he told of killing people took place in towns that hadn't had a single murder in ages. Most of the stories seemed to end either with him getting a lot of diamonds from his victims or with him taking another job washing dishes for sixteen hours a day at a rate of roughly a nickel an hour.

Spencer may have thought he was that big of a jerk, but if most of his crimes had happened it all, they had happened only in his mind as he sat safely tucked away in an opium den. He was an opium fiend.

It's difficult not to picture the veteran cops gathered around Spencer as he made his confession, trying not to laugh and eager to hear what yarn he'd spin next. For the most part, this was just the breakdown of an "opium slave deprived of the drug," and they could tell. They'd seen this sort of thing before. Still, at least a few of his stories checked out.

On a couple of occasions, Captain Halpin drove Spencer around town, and Spencer gleefully pointed out one spot after another. "I ransacked that house there," he said, pointing to 110 South Leavitt. "I paid the woman for my room, and when she was absent I took the money I paid her, besides what she left lying around. She was such a nice old lady. I guess that's the reason I didn't use my hammer on her."

Wasn't that nice of him?

At one point, a woman named Dora Schramm was brought to him.

"Do you know this woman?" they asked.

"Sure, I know her," Spender said. "I'd have sworn I killed that woman!"

Dora shrieked and fainted. Spencer *had* knocked her out cold with a hammer, then run off when her daughter came into the room. But she was alive. "What a skull that woman must have," said an awed Spencer, while the terrified Mrs. Schramm was revived.

Though they were able to establish that he was certainly a hold-up man, and that he was known to beat his victims into submission with a hammer, almost none of the murder stories really checked out. But then, only one of them had to, and the murder he'd been arrested for, that of Mildred Rexroat, a dancer, was enough.

Spencer had come from hard circumstances. Born Henry Skarupa, he had grown up in a West Side tenement, where his father was a thrice-married alcoholic given to "periods of insanity." In one of those periods, he had killed himself. Harry's brother, his only friend, killed himself shortly thereafter. His stepmother died around the same time, and Harry was sent to a charitable institution. His memories of his life at the cheerily named Home for the Friendless at 20th and Wabash were about the earliest clear memories he possessed. He ran away from there to work as a newsboy and was eventually arrested for stealing a suit of clothes and sent out to serve his first sentence at Joliet. Upon his being sent away, his sister Eva killed herself.

When he was finally released, he was a young man with few prospects and a grudge against the world that it's hard not to sympathize with. With no friends and little family that hadn't already committed suicide, Spencer went on a long spree as a robber and petty thug.

By the autumn of 1913, Harry was living in a rented room near 32nd and Rhodes, smack in the middle of the remains of Camp Douglas, the old Confederate prison that had sat on the Near South Side fifty years earlier.

In September of that year, he met Mrs. Mildred Rexroat, a dancer, and told her he'd arranged to get her a professional job teaching tango out in the suburbs. The two of them took an electric train out to Elgin, where they got off because he told her he wanted to show her a farm that his father had left to him. He led her under a viaduct, and shortly after they passed beneath it, he casually pulled out a revolver and shot her in the jaw. When she fell, presumably lifeless, to the ground, he beat her head in with a hammer, then shimmied the diamond ring from her finger and left the corpse on the railroad tracks, where railroad workers found it shortly thereafter.

He showed off the diamond ring to the Pattersons, a couple of friends of his back in Chicago, and the friends began to get suspicious that Spencer wasn't the nice guy he seemed to be. One day, he took Mrs. Patterson to a moving-picture show on State Street, then to a chop suey restaurant, and told her he knew that they knew he was a crook. "Now, you and Patterson ain't no fools," he said. "And if you say a word about this I will send you both the same route."

The next time Spencer went to the Patterson's flat, the police were lying in wait. He was arrested without putting up a fight, and immediately confessed to the murder—and practically every other crime that had ever been committed in the city.

"I'm tired of spending my time in the penitentiary," he said. "I would rather die than be sent there again."

He began lobbying to be hanged at once, and insisted on representing himself in court, but the judge told him he couldn't be hanged on his "own bare word." When Spencer pleaded guilty, the judge ordered the clerk to enter the plea as "not guilty" and appoint a defense attorney for him.

"You are charged," he was told, "with the most heinous crime ever committed in this county."

"There's other counties and other crimes," he sneered, interrupting. "All I did here was a common murder for robbery. I'm entitled to a rope around my neck."

He was taken to DuPage County to be tried. Naturally, his defense tried to claim he was insane. He was rude to witnesses during the trial, frequently shouting at them and insulting them.

His favorite insult, several sources noted, was "bonehead." The *Tribune* said that he used that name a hundred times a day as he sat in the court.

"Bonehead!" he shouted. "Go out and frame up. Ask the judge to tell you some law, you bonehead. You bonehead, you don't know anything. Get some more witnesses, you bonehead."

He insisted that he was not insane, but he sure seemed to be acting as though he was.

Pointing at one of the justices at one point, he shouted "For two bones they [will] string him up there, and you will have a nice necktie party, and you are all invited. I will tell you all about the fifty murders they have got me down for—fifty of them. Drink their blood. Just kill them for their blood —nothing else. Anything that anybody says, that is all right. Just tell it to the jury."

It may have been that all of his confessions were just an attempt to look insane—a trick that practically every prisoner facing the gallows tried at one point. He succeeded in getting the hanging delayed; he was originally convicted and sentenced to hang in December, less than three months after the crime was committed, but appeals allowed him to push the date back to July 31.

"How's the gallows?" Spencer asked the sheriff early on.

"Don't know," said the sheriff. "I never tried it."

"Oh, say, that won't do," said Spencer. "I don't want to take chances being hanged on a rotten old gallows like that. Why, the thing's all worm-eaten, like as not. I don't want you to have to hang me twice."

On July 30, he spent time watching the workmen erect the gallows where he would die, then sat listening to phonographs to cover the sound of the sandbags being hung. Jailers often hung huge bags of sand to get the "spring" out of the rope, and this would be the first hanging at the suburban prison in over half a century, so it required some testing.

He kept up his insistence that he was getting what he wanted. "I am perfectly happy in the certainty that I am to be hanged next Friday," he said. "I'm glad these lawyers have got to the end of their rope. Get it? 'End of their rope?' I don't want any commutation of my sentence. I'm tired of jail life."

He got his wish the next morning.

Spencer drew a rotten hand in life, and it's hard not to feel sorry for him. But he was certainly a jerk. We'll never truly know just how many people he actually killed; though several of the twenty-eight he confessed to were disproven, several more weren't, and more than one woman came forward to identify him as the man who had *attempted* to murder her. The police were convinced he'd killed at least four.

Just one is more than enough to qualify him as a jerk.

CHAPTER 18

Charles Comiskey
The Ego That Blackened America's Pastime

The 1919 "Black Sox" scandal nearly destroyed baseball. When it came out that the World Series, the most sacred of all secular American rituals at the time, had been "thrown" by White Sox players who had taken money from gamblers to lose on purpose, the nation was shocked and betrayed. Though gambling in baseball had always been widespread, and gamblers had been influencing the game quite openly since the game's earliest days, this was a scandal that rocked the game to its core.

Baseball had been considered "America's Pastime" since the days of the Civil War, when the soldiers marching across the country helped spread the game beyond its early strongholds in New York and Chicago. And now there was a stain that could never be washed away.

And it came from Chicago, of all places.

Chicago had long been a baseball town, one of the first cities where the sport really took hold in the days before the Civil War. During the run-up to the 1860 election, an exhibition match was played in Chicago between supporters of two rival candidates for president—Stephen Douglas and Abraham Lincoln. The Douglas men won handily, though papers reporting on the match cheerfully pointed out that it probably wouldn't actually affect the election much in the end.

Charles Comiskey, the White Sox manager, had taken the loss of the World Series in stride. "Chicago is the greatest of all baseball cities," he proudly told G. W. Axelson, a writer who was writing Comiskey's biography. "I make no exception, though I have been treated well wherever I've been. It's the greatest city because the fans will stick to a loser season after season."

Made in 1919, this may be one of the most astute statements made on Chicago sports. It was made shortly after his own team had won the pennant, and only a decade or so after the era when the Chicago Cubs had dominated the National League, taking back-to-back World Series titles of their own in 1907 and 1908. The White Sox had won the Series in 1906, then again eleven years later in 1917.

But the Sox would not go on to the World Series again for another forty years, wouldn't actually win the Series again until 2005, and would never again win one at the stadium that bore Comiskey's name. The Cubs, to date, have *still* not won another World Series since 1908, or even played in one since 1945. Most of the Chicago fans Comiskey spoke of would never live to see their favorite team win the Series at all. But, as he predicted, they stayed loyal, packing Comiskey Park and Wrigley Field season after season, hoping that the annual "Wait Til Next Year" threats would finally come true.

In that same talk with his biographer, Comiskey went on to speak about why baseball had become the national pastime. "The reason for the popularity of the sport is that it fits in with the temperament of the American people and because it is on the square. Everything is done in the open. What the magnates do behind the screens the fans care nothing about."

While Comiskey was right about Chicago fandom, he apparently didn't yet realize that his team had just lost the Series on purpose after gamblers paid them to do so.

When the scandal broke the next year, people jumped all over themselves to condemn the players.

What few seemed to say, though, was that the real problem may have been that Charles Comiskey, owner of the White Sox, was a complete jerk. Even if the fans truly didn't care about what happened "behind the screens," the players certainly did.

Charles "The Old Roman" Comiskey was born in 1859, just before the Civil War, making him one of the first generation who had grown up with baseball as a national sport (which is what

Charles Comiskey, looking not unlike Elvis's manager

people began to call it after the Civil War, when it spread to soldiers and grew outside of its early urban strongholds), and one of the children who survived the Great Chicago Fire in 1871. His father was an alderman for the Seventh Ward and known to his constituents as "Honest John Comiskey."

It was Honest John who was given the task of supervising the rebuilding of city hall after the original structure was largely destroyed by the fire. During this construction, he sent his son, young Charles, out to pick up a load of bricks. Hours passed, but Charles never returned.

A furious Honest John began to walk from the construction site to the brick site, retracing the route his son would have taken. He eventually found his brick wagon sitting, driverless, beside the road. It had been parked across the street from a baseball diamond, where Charles was standing on the pitcher's mound, throwing curve balls past one frustrated batter after another. He had paused to watch a game, witnessed a pitcher being crushed, and offered to step in to take care of things himself.

That's the way the story goes, anyway. It's difficult to imagine that they'd just let some kid walk onto the mound and take over— though the fact that he was the alderman's son may have helped. In any case, Charles could pitch like a pro. Honest John himself was impressed enough with his son's work on the field that he got into the wagon and finished the brick delivery himself, leaving his son to the game.

Over time, this story took on mythic proportions. Some say that this was the first time young Charles had ever played the game at all, and that passing that game in his brick wagon changed the course of baseball forever.

In any case, Chicago in those days was host to a number of semi-pro teams such as the Libertys, the Dreadnoughts, the Actives, the Mutuals, and the Never Sweat (who probably regretted picking such a name in July). There was plenty of opportunity for young "Commy" to sharpen his skills. In 1876 he began making fifty dollars a month playing professionally for a Milwaukee team.

By his mid-twenties he was not only playing professionally for the St. Louis Browns, but managing them, as well—and successfully. The Browns won several consecutive championships, and Comiskey went on to be a player-manager for several other teams, including an early Chicago pro team, the Chicago Pirates. Over a twelve-year career in the majors he maintained a respectable career batting average in the .260s and hit a career total of twenty-nine home runs (a fairly large number for the time, when homers were a very rare thing)[6]. In 1894 he bought a Western League club and became the owner of the Saint Paul Saints. In 1900, the team joined the American League, changed its name to the White Stockings, and moved to the South Side of Chicago.

Comiskey would own the White Sox for the rest of his life, seeing them through several pennants and the construction of the ballpark that bore his name. At the time, he was the only man in the history of baseball to rise from being a player to owning a team of his own.

Of course, anyone who builds a giant stadium and decides to put his own name on it is going to have quite an ego. And sometimes an ego like that can also be a sign of being a jerk.

Players in those days had no union, and there was no such thing as free agency. Professional baseball players were essentially slaves to the men who owned the teams, and few people ever took such unfair advantage of this as Charles Comiskey.

By the late 1910s, the White Sox were such a powerhouse in baseball that people began to accuse Comiskey of using his considerable power in the league to influence the outcome of games. "Occasionally," he said, "I have been charged with the crime of 'buying' pennants. If I am guilty, it has been for the sake of those who furnished the money. My friends wanted me to have a winner. The fans have insisted upon it. The winning of individual ballgames contributes to the total, and without more victories at the end of the season than anyone else there would have been no championships."

---

6 This season, in fact, marks the end of the "dead ball era," when home runs were rare. The league leader hit twelve of them in 1919. In 1920, Babe Ruth would stun the world by launching fifty-four homers.

In that particular long-winded statement, he doesn't exactly deny anything. However, when one thinks of a baseball club owner "buying" a pennant today, we usually imagine that they're attracting the best players to the club by luring them away with more money than a smaller team can afford.

Comiskey, though, was hardly a big spender. He may have built "the baseball palace of the world" at considerable expense, but he wasn't spending any more money than he had to on salaries. In fact, though his team was by most accounts the best in the league, his pay scale was abysmal. While Ty Cobb made twenty thousand dollars a year playing for Detroit, White Sox star "Shoeless Joe" Jackson was making only six thousand dollars (though Comiskey claimed that he was paying him ten thousand in order to save face). Player salaries were determined by Comiskey, and Comiskey alone. There was no discussion and his decisions could not be appealed. Players got three dollars per day for meals on away games while players from other teams got a dollar more, and a further fifty cents per game was deducted from their salaries as a fee for having the uniforms cleaned. When the players sent their manager to negotiate, Comiskey became bitter and spiteful.

In 1917, when the team won the World Series, the players' share of the World Series money should have been just under two thousand dollars a man, but Comiskey paid them only fifteen hundred dollars. Further enraging them, he had promised them all a bonus if they won the Series. The players all seem to have understood that this would be a cash reward and knew that Comiskey could spend money when he felt like it—he hosted plenty of lavish parties for his friends and the press. But when they won the Series, the "bonus" turned out to be a case of champagne. Adding insult to injury, it wasn't even good champagne. Ring Lardner, one of the furious players, said that "it tasted like stale piss."

The players' bitterness continued into 1919, and, according to one particularly damning legend, Comiskey's moves toward the players became particularly spiteful. In that season, he offered pitcher Eddie Cicotte a large bonus—perhaps as much as ten thousand dollars—if he won thirty games. When Cicotte reached twenty-eight wins, with two more easily in sight, he was mysteriously benched. Rumors swirled, and continue to swirl, that Comiskey had ordered Kid Gleason, the manager, to hold Cicotte out for the rest of the season to avoid having to pay the bonus. While no direct evidence has been found (the truth could only be known to Gleason himself), the players certainly seem to have thought that this was what happened, and relatives of Cicotte have said that movie scenes depicting Cicotte being denied the bonus he was about to earn were completely accurate.

Records indicate that Cicotte did, indeed, sit out for the last two weeks of the 1919 season. The only part of the story that doesn't ring true is the very notion that Comiskey would have ever offered anyone that kind of money as a bonus in the first place. If he had made the offer at all, it probably would have been as a joking offer of a reward he never imagined he might have to pay—Cicotte had never even won twenty games in a year before, and thirty-game winners were rare in those days.

Researching the incident today, the most likely scenario is that Comiskey offered the bonus as a joke, in passing, and Cicotte took him up on it. History is full of stories of jerks playing this sort of crooked game. Thomas Edison, for instance, offered young Nikola Tesla a fortune if he could find a way to improve the form of electricity he was providing his customers. When Tesla did exactly that and came to collect, Edison brushed him off, saying, "When you're fully American, you'll understand an American joke." Tesla was so mad that he quit and became a ditch digger for a while before Westinghouse bought him up and used his expertise to make Edison's direct-current brand of electricity obsolete.

Cicotte, too, would get his revenge. When the players met with gamblers to make arrangements, he was one of the ones who took the money. When the story eventually broke, it was Cicotte who reportedly went to Comiskey's house and informed him that the rumors were true. "I have played a crooked game," he's said to have said. "And I have lost."

Though the two teams seem reasonably well-matched if one reads the statistics, sports writers of the time generally seem to have considered the Sox to be the superior team. The Sox were slightly better on offense (their top three home-run hitters hit a combined total of eighteen home runs that year, compared to eleven for the Reds), and the Reds faired slightly better on defense.

The Cincinnati fans, however, had never had a World Series of their own. The owners expanded seating, adding left-field bleachers for the first time. Hotel accommodations became so scarce that fans were allowed to sleep on the benches in the park. Rumors that the Series was fixed were already going around—one Reds pitcher named Heller had reportedly turned down a five-thousand-dollar offer to lose a game on purpose. It's tempting to imagine what might have happened if *both* teams had agreed to throw the Series. Heller, however, proudly turned them down. "I told him to get out of my sight," he said. "If I ever saw him again, I'd beat him up."

Other Reds players showed similar swagger. "They knew better than to ask me," said center fielder Edd Roush. "I would have knocked the hell out of them. And they knew that, too."

Eight members of the Sox, however, were taking mysterious meetings at the Hotel Stinton, where they had checked in. Cicotte and another player had previously met with a couple of gamblers with an offer to throw the Series for one hundred thousand dollars, if the gamblers could come up with that kind of money. They'd taken meetings off and on ever since as the gamblers tried to get the financing in order. In Cicotte's hotel room on the night before the Series began, it's said that the gamblers offered the eight men twenty thousand dollars for each of the five games they lost, an amount that would come to more than ten thousand dollars a man if the Series was thrown. This was far more than Comiskey was paying most of them.

Comiskey, for his part, had already gotten wind of a fix, by all accounts. One New York sportswriter supposedly overheard Joe Jackson begging "Commy" to keep him out of the first game—he had heard rumors of the fix and wanted no part of it.

To what extent the Series was actually thrown is up to some debate—whether Shoeless Joe was truly in on the fix, or just took some money despite playing his best—has never really been established. By one account, the players threw the first game (in which they were trounced 9–1), then, when they didn't see any money, played their hardest the rest of the Series. In any case, they lost to the Reds in the end.

Rumors about the fix began to circulate during the next season, while the Sox fought toe-to-toe with the Cleveland Indians for the pennant. By September, the chatter had gotten loud enough that a grand jury was called to investigate, and both Cicotte and Jackson confessed their part in the scheme. Unfortunately for Sox fans, the admission came right at the end of the season, when the Sox were locked in a tight pennant race. Comiskey suspended all seven players named as conspirators at once, gutting his team and probably costing them the pennant. They finished the season two games behind the Indians.

By the end of 1921, eight players had been banned from the sport for life, and baseball's reputation as a "fair" sport took a while to recover (if indeed it ever did). Comiskey, though, was inducted into the baseball Hall of Fame in 1939.

CHAPTER 19

James Colosimo
The Grandfather of the Mob, A Kingpin of Vice

In 1920, a group of men gathered at Patrick O'Malley's saloon at Clark and Polk to reminisce about the nights when James "Big Jim" Colosimo sat at the bar playing pinochle with the other regulars. Across the street stood a basement bakery where Colosimo had slept many nights when he was too poor even to pay for a night in a flophouse, back in the days before he became one of the kingpins of the Levee District. O'Malley himself presided over the scene, stroking his chin and saying, "one by one the roses fall."

Early that evening, Big Jim had been found shot to death in his South Side restaurant. There were no witnesses, but many men and women with motives for killing him were crawling through the city—rival vice lords, ex-wives with grudges, and others who felt that the world would be a better place with Big Jim out of the way. Prohibition, the law banning the sale of alcohol, had gone into effect less than four months before. This had changed everything for crime and vice in the city, and the organized crime world—which Colosimo had basically founded on his own—was realigning itself. Some of the "old guard" simply had to go to make room for the new bosses.

Colosimo was one of the first major casualties. The identity of the killer was never found out; when his wife was asked if she suspected anyone, she replied, "I should say that I suspect *everybody*." Colosimo had been alone in the restaurant when an unknown gunman stepped from the cloakroom, shot him to death, and left undetected, not even taking Jim's diamond cuff links as he left. Obviously, this had been no random robbery. This was a hit, plain and simple.

There's probably some sort of cosmic force in the universe that dictates that somewhere in the annals of Chicago organized crime and political rackets, there simply *must* be a guy named "Big Jim." In fact, there were a couple of them: Big Jim Colosimo, the grandfather of the Chicago mob, and Big Jim O'Leary, a gambling magnate. They lived at roughly the same time and presumably met from time to time—indeed, O'Leary was said to be working with Colosimo early in the Prohibition days and was one of the suspects in his murder.

Big Jim O'Leary got off to a rather notorious start in the city—his mother was Catherine O'Leary, the infamous Mrs. O'Leary that the *Chicago Times* blamed for the Great Chicago Fire in 1871. Both Jim and his mother developed a lifelong hatred of reporters (for fairly obvious reasons). By 1909 "Big Jim," just a boy during the fire, was running a saloon in the stockyards in addition to running various gambling operations. He suspended his hatred of reporters to make a statement in 1909, when a story circulated that the *true* origin of the fire was a bunch of kids sneaking into the O'Leary barn to milk the cow in order to get some milk to make whiskey punch, and who accidentally started a fire.

Standing behind the bar, O'Leary put his thumbs into the armholes of his vest and proceeded to tell his own version of the story, which he said had never been in print. "I don't care what anybody else says about the fire," he said. "My parents are dead and can't defend themselves against this latest fake as to the origin of the fire, but I'll speak out, and plainly, too. That story about the cow kicking over the lamp was the monumental fake of the century. I know what I'm talking about when I say that the fire was caused by spontaneous combustion in the hayloft.

"You see," he went on, "it was like this: The old man had put in a load of 'green' hay a few days before the fire. Below the hayloft were the stables where the cows were kept. We had several cows and did quite a milk business. . . . both my father and mother went to their graves sad at heart over the world wide notoriety given them in the printed accounts of the burning of Chicago. I wish to

Original ad for Dale singing at Colosimo's café
LIBRARY OF CONGRESS

make it as emphatic as possible that the O'Leary cow[7] did not kick over a lamp."

Big Jim O'Leary does not seem to have been particularly jerky, as gambling kingpins go. And if he was bitter and cynical about the world, he could hardly be blamed. In fact, that he crawled up from such smoldering wreckage to carve out a name for himself is really rather admirable.

Big Jim Colosimo, too, pulled himself up by the bootstraps. In a few short years he went from being a regular street pickpocket to being one of the most notorious vice lords in the city—at the same time as being a respected local politician (to the extent that such people are respected at all) and a restaurateur. He strutted around the town wearing diamond rings and organizing the petty thugs and scoundrels in the city to keep them in line. When "organized" crime was still a fairly new concept, Colosimo created something akin to order out of pure chaos.

Colosimo arrived in Chicago some time around the late nineteenth century (reports differ) and cut his teeth in the world of low-level vice, pulling pickpocketing jobs while he worked as a newsboy and a boot black. Along the way, he caught the eye of Bathhouse John Coughlin and Hinky Dink Kenna, the notorious aldermen of the Levee District. By 1900, he was a precinct captain himself, acting as a sort of liaison between Chicago politics and the booming "resort district" around 22nd Street, which was teeming with fancy restaurants and fancier brothels in between the usual flophouses, whorehouses, taverns, and dens. The line between the upscale and low-level places got blurry from time to time; one brothel had both a one-dollar entrance and a twenty-five-cent entrance. Both doors led to the same girls.

Having risen to prominence in such a place, Colosimo took a liking to diamonds and fancy white suits, strutting around in enough of them to be called Diamond Jim as well as Big Jim (and there was also a second Diamond Jim floating around town; he would eventually be present at Colosimo's funeral).

---

7 The cow itself was reported in the *Tribune* to have been served up as oxtail soup in a restaurant a few months after the fire.

In 1900 Colosimo married a woman named Victoria Moresco and opened a "resort" of his own that made him even richer. Though new politicians would come through town promising reform, and even to clean up the Levee, Colosimo seemed to survive every sweep. His taste and sense of humor were legendary—even years after his death, old customers in Chicago taverns were still retelling the story of the time Colosimo found a wonderful green cloth and took it to the nearest tailor to have a suit made.

The tailor told him he couldn't make a suit from that sort of material. "That," he said, "is pool table cloth."

"Make up the suits," Colosimo said.[8]

The suits were made. You didn't say no to Big Jim.

And the suit looked fine on him—but didn't work out so well for his friend. His friend wore the suit on St. Patrick's Day, got into an argument with a man over whether St. Patrick was Italian, and ended up stabbing the man to death. The green suit made him awfully easy to find as he tried to make his getaway.

While he grew in power, Big Jim's tastes became more refined. He was a noted patron of the opera, and his cafe, Colosimo's, became more and more elegant. Soon, it was actually noted for its high-class food and wine. Even criminals were kept to a strict code of behavior there. The piano player was replaced with a full orchestra, and the city's cultural elite began to be seen there. As the *Tribune* later summed things up, "the professor at the piano was replaced by a fine orchestra and 'Izzy the Rat' [the piano player] had to give up his seat for such men as Tita Ruffa, the opera singer."

When new laws dictated that Colosimo's had to close at one o'clock in the morning, Colosimo opened another room next door. When closing time came, he would simply shuffle the patrons into the next room and keep serving drinks all night. As his fortune grew he spent lavishly—he began to take an orchestra with him when he vacationed in Hot Springs during the brutal Chicago winters.

---

8 It may be that Bathhouse John took fashion advice from Big Jim; he, too, was known to go around in suits made of pool-table cloth.

But the connections he made and affairs he carried on during these wild years would soon pile up on him, making him a lot of enemies. By the time of his murder, it did, indeed, seem like *everybody* was a suspect.

Big Jim always had an appetite for women, and his success took a toll on his first marriage. "While they were struggling they were happy," said one of his wife's sisters, "but when money came it brought only unhappiness. They were happy until about four years ago (ca. 1916), when my sister told me she believed her husband was not true to her."

Indeed, Colosimo was living with another woman by then. Having reached middle age and a good deal of success, he had decided, like so many before him, to celebrate his status with a new pretty young wife. A woman named Dale Winter had come to his cafe as an entertainer recruited by her boyfriend, violinist Arthur Fabbri. With help from a music teacher hired by Colosimo, she was soon the featured attraction at the cafe, and Jim took to giving her extravagant gifts of money and jewels. Fabbri couldn't possibly compete. The Levee was soon abuzz with gossip that Big Jim and Dale were now an item, and neighbors reported that they could hear Jim fighting with Victoria, his wife, from outside.

When Victoria found out about Dale, she took her money and jewels (which, combined, were worth about seventy-five thousand dollars) and took off. Colosimo filed a divorce bill, which was granted by default when Victoria didn't show up in court. Jim finally married Dale in March 1920. Regulars at the cafe toasted her as "Little Mrs. Big Jim."

But the union would be cut short by Jim's murder after barely two months, and both the first Mrs. Colosimo and the jilted Mr. Fabbri made the list of suspects.

More likely, though, was that the murder was the first shot in the gang war that would consume the city for the next couple of decades.

Black Hand gangsters—a loosely organized band of extortionists—had always met in Colosimo's place, and he had always been happy to let them, until they tried to extort two thousand dollars from one of his friends. That time, he tipped another gang of Black Handers off, and three were killed in the ensuing scuffle. To some, this made Colosimo a pioneer in the field of hiring gunmen to do his dirty work. But rumors went around that the betrayed gang now considered Colosimo a marked man.

Meanwhile, it had been expected that Colosimo would contribute a lot of money to the defense fund for one Jimmy Vinci, who was on trial for the murder of Mossy Enright, a fellow racketeer. He didn't, and that, too, might have made him a target.

But for all of this, the loudest whispers were to do with the growing gang warfare. In January, Prohibition had become the law of the land, and gangsters were chomping at the bit to become the city's chosen purveyors of bootleg liquor. One of the biggest leaders to emerge was Johnny Torrio, a former New York thug who had learned to apply an element of refinement to the brutal techniques he'd learned as a member of the notorious Five Points Gang.

It was Colosimo who brought Torrio to Chicago in the first place. At the time, he was being hounded by blackmailers and needed a henchman who could quiet them down. Torrio was an expert in shutting blackmailers up—sometimes making sure they'd never breathe another breath, let alone utter another threat.

This was the period where Colosimo was using his friendliness with Chicago politicians to organize all of the vice into the one "syndicate," and Torrio became the frontman and chief enforcer for Colosimo, going out to do his dirty work for him. He was a brutal man but played his role with such manners and courtesy that the thugs referred to him as "Nice Johnny."

Torrio did his job well—too well. Soon, he had outgrown Big Jim. He was rolling in money, and the city officials were far more afraid of him, personally, than he was of them. And when Prohibition came, he quickly realized that there was a lot more money to be made in bootleg liquor than in simple prostitution and extortion rackets.

But Colosimo was still the boss. In 1919, he and Torrio opened a resort of their own, The Four Deuces, at 2222 South Wabash.

Colosimo's awesome tomb at Oak Woods Cemetery
PHOTO BY AUTHOR

And, according to one theory, Colosimo had refused, for some reason (perhaps because his new wife, who was also a choir singer, didn't want him involved in such vice), to let his men become involved in bootleg liquor. With only Big Jim holding him back from fabulous wealth, Torrio had a pretty clear motive to get Big Jim out of the way.

There was never an "official" suspect to Colosimo's murder, and no witnesses, other than a porter who had seen a man in a long gray overcoat and a soft black hat pacing about the sidewalk in front of Colosimo's place. This was hardly a good lead; half the men in Chicago answered the description given.

Some said that Torrio brought in a man named Frankie Yale to pull the trigger on Big Jim.

Other suspected none other than Big Jim O'Leary, who was also working with Torrio at the time.

And some said that the trigger man was Torrio's young lieutenant, with whom he would take over Colosimo's empire and effectively take over the city in the coming years: a twenty-one-year-old kid named Al Capone.

CHAPTER 20
Tillie Klimek
The Black Widow of Little Poland

When crime buffs speak of Tillie Klimek at all these days, they tend to speak of her as "the psychic serial killer," who, in addition to her prowess as a murderess, was known to predict the deaths of her friends and relatives as a young girl, then claimed to have precognitive dreams "predicting" the deaths of her victims as an adult.

The "psychic" angle was probably invented by pulp magazine writers: I've never found any mention of her claiming to have any sort of supernatural powers in her lifetime. But there's a kernel of truth behind it; one day, she announced to her husband, Joe, that he was going to die in a few days.

"But I'm only sick," said the confused man. "I'll be better soon."

"No," Tillie cheerfully told him. "You're going to die in a few days."

As he lay in his bed the next day, Tillie came into his room to announce the wonderful bargain she'd found—she'd bought him a coffin for only thirty dollars, and it was now stashed in their basement with the permission of the landlord. The landlord would eventually deny this, but Joe was in no shape to go down to the basement to check.

Tillie's "prediction" came true—her husband died a few days later.

But this was no psychic trick on her part. She knew perfectly well that he was going to die, because she was the one who had had poisoned him.

And she knew only too well what arsenic could do. This was not her first marriage, and, as a killer, this was not her first rodeo.

She wasn't trying to be a psychic by telling him he would die soon. She was just being a jerk.

The house where Tillie killed her last victim is still standing on Winchester Street. She and her next-to-last husband occupied the third floor.
PHOTO BY AUTHOR

Lots of writers, from 1904 to the present, have enjoyed trying to play "connect the dots" to connect Johann Hoch, the early twentieth-century bluebeard, to H. H. Holmes, whose career was coming to an end right around the time Hoch arrived in America. But I'd be happier if we could connect him to Otillie Gburek-Mitkiewicz-Ruskowski-Kupszyk-Klimek, whose career began a few years later. Like Hoch, she seemed to be in the habit of murdering her spouses with arsenic shortly after the wedding took place. Imagine what might have happened if the two of them had gotten together; surely they would have tried to poison one another. It's a black comedy waiting to happen!

Though a couple of recent TV profiles have revived her somewhat, for decades Tillie Klimek was a forgotten serial killer. But if the stories about her were true, she could have rivaled any other that the city saw. She could only ever be convicted of one murder, that of her fourth husband, but police suspected her of many more.

According to stories that circulated, her husbands weren't the only people she was suspected of killing—friends and family were known to die after dining at her house. Some of the wilder stories even claimed that she was the head of a "Bluebeard Clique" that operated in Little Poland and was headquartered at her house, 924 North Winchester (which, unlike practically every other serial killer's house in town, is still standing—residents have half-jokingly referred to it as "old lady Tillie Klimek's haunted house").

But how wild were the stories, really?

In October 1922, Joseph Klimek was admitted to the West Side hospital and was seen to be gravely ill. The doctors suspected arsenic poisoning, and when tests proved them right, they arrested Tillie, his wife of a little over a year, and her son. They were a bit disturbed right off the bat to find that she'd been married many times before. Her first husband, Joseph Mitkiewicz, had been dead for around twenty years, but in the last few years, she'd been married at least four more times. Each husband had quickly died.

Like Hoch before, Tillie Klimek was not the bombshell one would expect a professional marriage artist to be; she was a frumpy woman in her mid-forties at the time of her arrest. Reporter Genevieve Forbes described her as "a fat, squat, Polish peasant woman, forty-five years old but looking fifty-five, with a lumpy figure, capacious hands and feet, and dull brown hair skinned back in a knot at the back of her head." Though she'd lived in the United States since she was a baby, she spoke only broken English. This set her apart from many of the women who'd been accused of murder in Illinois. The hit musical *Chicago,* in which a woman beats a murder rap by being attractive, was not entirely fiction—it was based on a true story and a real issue that came up at the time. Seven out of nine women accused of murder in Illinois in the early twentieth century were acquitted, and it seemed to be impossible to convict a young, attractive woman. Tillie, who was neither young nor attractive, probably never stood a chance in court.

But the evidence against her was pretty damning, anyway.

Four months before her arrest, she had asked Joseph, her new husband, if he was insured. He said that he carried one thousand dollars from the Catholic Order of Foresters, but she told him to drop it. She replaced it by taking out *two* life insurance policies, plus an accident policy, on his life. She told him, apparently quite cheerfully, that he wouldn't live much longer.

Soon after, he became ill.

For days, he told his doctors, she had greeted him in the morning with remarks like, "You are pretty near dead now!" and "Didn't I tell you, you aren't going to live long?"

When asked, Tillie admitted that she'd given Joseph some mysterious "white powder" that she'd acquired from a neighbor, her cousin Nellie Koulek, who, herself, was arrested. According to *her* story, Mrs. Klimek had told her she was tired of her husband, and she suggested a divorce.

"I know of a better way," Tillie said. "Do you have any poison?"

"I told her that all I had was some rat poison," Mrs. Koulek said. "And she told me to give her some. She didn't say what she was going to do with it, however, and I had no idea that she intended to poison her husband."

The body of Frank Kupszyk, one of her previous husbands, was disinterred and found to contain "enough arsenic to kill four men," according to the police. Another of her dead husbands, and one of Mrs. Koulek's, were quickly disinterred for testing. An anonymous letter had been sent to the police indicating that at least one of them was poisoned.

As he lay in bed, Joseph Klimek weakly announced that he'd press charges against Tillie, who responded by kissing him.

In the next week, the police began to find more and more about Mrs. Klimek. New husbands—all dead—kept being discovered. One of her cousins reported that his sister had died mysteriously after eating at Mrs. Klimek's house. Another cousin said the same thing had happened to one of her brothers and two of her sisters.

Particularly damning were stories told by neighbors who lived near Tillie and her previous husband, Frank Kupszyk, at 924 North Winchester. Tillie, it seemed, had told many people that Frank was sick and "would not live long," and had even gone out and purchased a thirty-dollar bargain coffin, which she supposedly kept in the basement. She had sat beside his bed sewing her mourning hat and dress. When he died, she played dance music on a phonograph that sat in the room with the corpse.

Throughout the early part of the ordeal after her arrest, Tillie betrayed little emotion (as would be her habit), until her still-living parents arrived to visit her. That made her launch into a long monologue that the *Tribune* described as follows (with Polish words translated and profane words deleted): "I didn't rob nobody; I didn't shoot nobody; I didn't kill nobody. I didn't! Everybody pick on me. Everybody makes eyes at me like they going to eat me. Why do they make eyes at me like that? I tell the truth. Anything I did I did to myself. Nobody else."

Soon, both Tillie and Nellie were being formally held, and *more* exhumations were being ordered; by this time it must have seemed as though half the graveyard was being dug up. There *did* seem to be several people in "the K cousins'" families who had died, including six of Nellie's nine children and one of her grandchildren (her remaining children fell all over themselves to accuse her of being a murderess). Practically every relative, neighbor, and friend who had quarreled with the women seemed to have died shortly thereafter. A couple of neighbors claimed that they'd become terribly sick after eating candy that Tillie had given them.

Before long it was being said that Tillie or Nellie might have actually been the "high priestess" of a whole "Bluebeard Clique" in their neighborhood, a few possible members of which were arrested (and later released). By Thanksgiving, police suspected Tillie and Nellie of having poisoned twenty people, fourteen of whom had died. Even a dog that had lived behind Tillie and Frank on Winchester Street, and who annoyed Tillie with its barking, was found to have died of arsenic poisoning.

"This is the most startling and intricate poison case to come to my attention the eighteen years I have been coroner," said Peter Hoffman. "There is no question that Mrs. Klimek poisoned every one she wished to get out of the way. Her victims may total a score." As it was, Hoffman had found arsenic in the bodies of four of Tillie's husbands—not counting Joseph, who was still clinging to life in the hospital.

In March of 1923 (by which time Joseph was expected to live, though he was still semi-paralyzed), Tillie was put on trial for the murder of her previous husband, Frank Kupszyk, and Nellie was on trial for providing the poison to her.

Genevieve Forbes, a reporter, was almost shocked at the extent to which the two women lacked the tools other "killer ladies" had employed to arouse the sympathy of the jury. "They are without guile or the aid of hairdresser, manicure, modiste or diary," she wrote. "They carry no vanity box, rouge, or lipstick. The upturned brims of their plain black hats are uncompromising and refuse to cast kind shadows over their faces. They don't bite their lips when in distress. They mop their brows with plain cotton handkerchiefs held in capacious hands. . . . the pathetically coquettish pearl dangling pin in Mrs. Koulek's hat seems a sardonic joke on the lined face beneath the hat."

In other words, there'd be no chance that the women could "give 'em the old razzle-dazzle." If they were to be acquitted, it would be on the weight of the evidence. And with arsenic found in the bodies of so many men, odds for Tillie seemed dim.

By Ms. Forbes's account, the trial was a "merry affair." Judge Kavanagh had to remind the audience that "this is not a theater" on several occasions as, one by one, physicians, chemists, nurses, and insurance agents were called to the witness stand. Some joked their way through the testimony to the delight of the spectators.

One grave digger, who was also a neighbor, said she'd seen Tillie kissing a man who wasn't her husband in the window of the house on Winchester.

"Then what happened?" asked the attorney.

"Why, then Tillie put up some newspapers in front of the window, so I couldn't see in!"

Tillie, and the rest of the court, giggled.

But the gravedigger, one Roman Urbanski, calmed down when he began speaking of his work exhuming the body of Tillie's first husband, describing how he had placed various parts of the body into jars as Tillie looked on, with a look Forbes described as "disturbingly gleeful."

One nurse testified as to Tillie's bedside manner as Joseph, her most recent husband, lay in the hospital.

"What did Mrs. Klimek say?" asked the attorney.

"She shouted at me: 'If he makes any trouble for you, take a two-by-four and hit him over the head with it!'"

Mrs. Klimek had smiled as the nurse made the two-by-four remark, but it still sounded pretty bad. And she finally lost her cool the next day, as a chemist revealed the results of his tests on the bodies of three of her husbands. The verdict every time: "Death due to arsenical poisoning." There were between eight and fourteen milligrams of arsenic in each body, but none in the soil surrounding the grave.

She was only on trial for the murder of one of the husbands, but evidence of other crimes continued to mount. One attorney told her that back in October, she'd asked where Mrs. Klimek had obtained arsenic, and she'd said that she'd gotten it from Mrs. Koulek, put it on some meat, and served it to Joseph when he was drinking.

The officer who had arrested her told a more ominous story—as he put her in the wagon, she had wagged her finger at him and said "the next one I want to cook a dinner for is you. You made all my trouble."

Her landlady from Winchester Street took the stand as well, and told of the day she had come home with news of the thirty-dollar coffin. Frank was only sick, then, not dead. "I told her," she said, "I chase you and the coffin out." She apparently relented, though, when told that Frank was dying.

Still another neighbor came and said that when Frank died, Tillie grabbed his corpse by the ear and shouted "You devil, you won't get up any more!"

When it came time for Tillie to take the stand herself, she wore a black dress and a black hat that she'd bought the day Frank died. She denied that she had killed Frank, and said that he had "died by moonshine." "I loved [my husbands]," she said. "And they loved me. They died same as other people. I not responsible for that. I could no help if they wanted to die." She further denied that she had bought Frank a coffin or played music on the day of his death.

On the day her verdict was to be announced, Genevieve Forbes allowed herself another chance to describe Tillie in unflattering terms, this time saying "[she] has a greasy complexion and a lumpy figure, growls instead of murmurs, and knows a crochet needle better than lipstick." She went on to detail all of the other four women who had been convicted of murder in Cook County. None, she noted, was any great beauty. It was only the pretty ones who got acquitted.

Tillie Klimek was found guilty after the jury deliberated for only an hour and twenty minutes. Four jurors had voted for the death penalty (a penalty never leveled against a woman in Chicago), but she was given life in prison—the longest prison sentence a woman had ever been given in Cook County. Tillie said nothing except to remark that it was warm back in her cell. She assumed the sentence would be overturned eventually, but despite a short series of appeals and new trials, it was always upheld.

"We have here a woman of average intelligence," said Judge Kavanagh (who meant it as a compliment), "a modern housewife and a good cook. When she is among women she is affectionate, and, it is said, she is the most popular woman in the jail. Yet, the testimony showed, cold bloodedly, without feeling or remorse, she killed three of her husbands and attempted to kill a fourth. If this woman was let loose today, she would kill another man. She has a desire to see men with whom she was intimate suffer." Kavanagh stopped short of endorsing the view that Tillie was the head of a "clique" of poisoners, but did suggest that she wasn't alone as a killer in Little Poland. "Criminologists tell us there are few such people on this earth," he said, "[but] I venture to say there are more husbands poisoned in this community than the police or authorities realize. But the knowledge that Tillie Klimek has 'gone down' will stay their hands."

Genevieve Forbes was now free to call Tillie "grewsomely cruel," and did so. But as "grewsomely cruel" as she'd been to her husbands (and, perhaps, neighbors and relatives), she was a different kind of cruel to Nellie Koulek, her cousin. Nellie was dismissed from the trial for supplying poison to kill Joseph Klimek, but was still suspected of killing her own previous husband and given a separate trial, which began a few months later.

During it, neighbors spoke of a "petting party" between Nellie and her husband, Albert Koulek, while she was still married to her previous husband Wojcik Sturmer, who, it was alleged, she had poisoned to free her to marry Albert. One neighbor said he had seen Albert and Nellie conducting "twilight loving parties" on her back porch, during which they would hug and sing songs to each other.

"And that was not all that I saw," said one neighbor. He claimed that Wojcik tried to chew Nellie out for carrying on with Albert, but that she had "used a broom" on him.

Nellie also had to sit through the fun of having three of her sons and one of her daughters take the stand to call her a killer. A daughter spoke of Albert getting drunk and beating her with a strap. Nellie herself only replied "never did" in a dull, sing-song voice, to every question put to her.

That trial ended in a hung jury; a retrial acquitted her. It's difficult to guess now whether Nellie was, in fact, a poisoner, or if all of the people connected to Nellie and Tillie were simply killed by Tillie herself, and that Tillie had set Nellie up to look guilty (when she was really just an awfully unpleasant woman to be around, which is not a federal offense).

During her trial, in addition to being condemned by her children, Nellie was described in the press as "a sexless bulk of worn, imitation seal coat, cotton stocking, plain green skirt, sunken gums, and hardened hands . . . a lump of a figure." Just making Nellie live through the trial and putting her in a position to be described in such terms in public would be jerky enough of Tillie, to say the least. Nellie didn't sit silently and mechanically through the trial—she was hysterical, often shrieking and crying in the courtroom, unable to comprehend much going on.

But Tillie didn't stop there; Judge Kavanagh later remembered that she would torment Nellie mercilessly in the cell.

One morning, when Nellie was about to be taken out of the cell, Tillie (who spoke better English than Nellie and had a better idea of what was going on) gave her a hug and whispered something in her ear that made her emit a blood-curdling scream. She broke away from the hug and began scratching at the cell doors, screaming for a priest and for her children.

What Tillie had whispered was, "Nellie, they are taking you out to hang you. They are only going to give me life imprisonment, because I have pull with the judge and the attorney. Good-bye, my poor cousin. I'll try to have your children taken care of."

Some said that this morbid sense of humor of Tillie's was the sole motive behind telling her husbands that they were going to die. But it was hard to argue with the evidence of arsenic being found in so many of them.

Tillie lived the rest of her life in prison, where she spent her time sewing American flags and was described as a model prisoner. She died of a heart ailment after thirteen years in prison at the age of fifty-eight.

One can imagine that Nellie probably did not visit her in her cell.

CHAPTER 21

Richard Loeb
The Not-So-Genius Killer

Years ago, when I was just a kid, I fell asleep listening to a Cubs game and woke up in the middle of the night with a talk program playing on the radio. An old man was being interviewed about his life and was saying something about how a couple of kids in town had planned to murder him when he was a boy.

"My death had been very carefully planned to take place after school," the old man said. "But I remembered that I had a dental appointment, so I wasn't where they expected me to be."

"So they did in your classmate?" asked the interviewer.

"So they did in my classmate," he confirmed. "Bobby Franks."

Years later, I learned that the man was Armand Deutsch, who had grown up to be a Hollywood producer and friend of Ronald Reagan. The way I imagined it at the time was that he had been a boy at a country schoolhouse (I thought all old men went to country schoolhouses when they were boys) who had nearly been murdered by a bunch of local yokels.

In fact, Deutsch was an affluent South Side kid who had been picked up to go to the dentist by his family's chauffeur. And in doing so, he had narrowly avoided becoming the victim of The Crime of the Century.

Chicago was a hotbed of crime for much of the twentieth century—a reputation it's never quite been able to shake. But the one they called The Crime of Century wasn't the execution of several gangsters in one fell swoop, a big political heist, or the spree of a serial killer. It was the solitary murder of fourteen-year-old Bobby Franks.

In May of 1930, Jacob Franks received a ransom letter demanding ten thousand dollars for the return of his son, Bobby, who had been kidnapped. He was preparing to make the pay-

Dear Sir:

Proceed immediately to the back
platform of the train. Watch the east side
of the track. Have your package ready. Look
for the first LARGE, RED, BRICK factory situated immediately adjoining the tracks on the
east. On top of this factory is a large, black
watertower with the word CHAMPION written on
it. Wait until you have COMPLETELY passed the
south end of the factory - count five very rap
idly and then IMMEDIATELY throw the package as
far east as you can.

Remember that this is your only
chance to recover your son.

Yours truly,

GEORGE JOHNSON

The ransom note

ment when Bobby's body was found in a railroad culvert under the Pennsylvania Line tracks near Wolf Lake. He was naked; the only clothing nearby was a sock that had belonged to him and a pair of odd eyeglasses that didn't. The boy appeared to have been killed with a blunt instrument, though none of the blows seemed bad enough that they should have been fatal. Some suggested that he had been strangled or killed with poison gas.

As the police and the public scoured the city for "clews" (as the *Tribune* persisted in spelling the word "clues") to the identity of the slayers, strange theories of desperate men (or even women) spread through the city, and a temporary "Crime Head-quarters" was established at the Drake Hotel by Robert Crowe, the state's attorney. Another girl disappeared that same week and was reported to have been kidnapped as well, though it turned out that she had just gone off on a "romantic adventure."

Nearly a week later, authorities were still saying that the case was just as mysterious as it had been on the first day. Jacob Franks, sixty-five years old and rich (he said he preferred real estate to golf), was naturally distraught, though he pointed out that Bobby would not have been pleased at all about the papers referring to him as a "little boy." He himself had always called him "baby," to which Bobby would say, "Don't you realize my age?"

He was sure that the killers had been someone that he and young Bobby had known and tortured himself as he thought of all of his friends, relatives, and acquaintances, wondering if they could have been the one who had killed his son.

Finally, at the end of May, two suspects were taken in: Richard Loeb and Nathan Leopold, two young college students. Loeb was a relative of Franks.

These arrests were a shock to both the Franks family and the city at large; both young men were far too well-off to be concerned with getting ransom money. And they were no lowlife criminals; in fact, by most accounts, they were geniuses. The year before, Richard Loeb had become the youngest person ever to graduate from the University of Michigan—he was only eighteen at the time, an age when most young men are just finishing high school. Nathan Leopold spoke something like two dozen languages and had an IQ in the low 200s. He had spent the days before and after the murder dealing with law exams.

At length, it came out that Loeb, bored with life and believing that the normal laws of man did not apply to geniuses such as him and his friend, had determined that the greatest intellectual thrill of all would be to kill a person, and to do so in such a way that the police would never find out. Leopold, who seems to have been hopelessly in love with Loeb, was persuaded to go along with the scheme.

And so the two hatched a plot: They would kill someone, dispose of the body, and send out a ransom note to cover their tracks. After discussing a few potential victims they thought Armand Deutsch would be a good target, but when he didn't show up where they expected him to, they settled on Bobby Franks. They picked him up after school in a car; since he knew them, he had no reason not to get in a car with them.

It was probably Loeb who struck the first blow with the chisel. According to later accounts, Leopold, disturbed at what they had done, went pale and said, "My God, this is terrible." But Loeb laughed over the corpse as they removed and burned Franks's clothes, then shoved him into the culvert.

For a couple of "geniuses," they bungled the crime pretty thoroughly. For one thing, Leopold left his glasses near the body. They had an unusual hinge mechanism that was available only at one eyeglass shop in Chicago, and only three pairs like them had been sold. The only customer who could have possibly been in town on the day of the murder was Leopold. They had also used a typewriter in Leopold's room to type the ransom letter. Typewriters were almost as good as fingerprints; you could almost always match a typewritten letter to the typewriter it was printed on. Leopold had discarded the machine, but admitted to having owned one.

In the "hot box," Leopold almost seemed to enjoy "matching wits" with the detectives as he claimed that he had lost the glasses while bird watching. (In addition to speaking fifteen languages at the time, he was a noted expert on ornithology.)

He and Loeb were kept in separate rooms as they were interrogated. Loeb is said to have claimed that if he was going to kill someone, Franks was exactly the snot-nosed brat he'd pick. On May 31, as the evidence piled up and the abandoned typewriter was discovered in the Jackson Park lagoon, both of them confessed at the same time to attorney Robert Crowe.

In their respective rooms in the Drake Hotel, where each was being held, each of them blamed the other for the killing, but both confessed that they had killed Bobby Franks for thrills.

Leopold now seemed passive and detached, but occasionally regretful. When they took him to the bridge where the typewriter had been dumped, he said he'd like to jump off it. When told that he'd never survive, he sadly said, "That would suit me just fine."

Loeb was something else. Initially, the papers described him as a "sure footed, well poised steeplejack, scaling the spires of a vagrant imagination and from them glancing downward to laugh at the clumsy efforts of policemen bent on learning who kidnapped and killed Robert Franks."

But as it became clear that he had *not* executed the "perfect crime," he lost a lot of his swagger. He continued to insist, "this will be the making of me," but his voice was trembling somewhat now.

Loeb tried to say that he was simply acting under Leopold's influence. One of his college sweethearts seemed to back this up, saying that she had been very close to "Dickie" Loeb until "Babe" Leopold had caused a rift between them. Loeb, it seemed, had been quite a ladies' man since he was only thirteen, "but girls who were fond of Nathan Leopold," wrote the papers, "girls who admit that they have been in love with 'Babe' Leopold, are not so easy to find."

Leopold claimed that it was Loeb who had been in control the whole time, and his version of the story was more convincing, if only because he seemed more coherent in his confession. He answered every question without bravado or profanity, and in great detail. He apparently believed that cooperating with police was his best chance.

Loeb, though, was having none of that. A week and a half into the investigation, he even claimed that Leopold had hypnotic powers over him, and that he had taken advantage of his own weaker intellect, further weakened by moonshine, to put him into a trance during which he was forced to go along with the bloody scheme.

A few of Leopold's classmates confirmed that he had demonstrated hypnosis and held séances at college, but these are more likely along the lines of tricks and pranks. He had "hypnotized" a student into drinking something nasty (castor oil or dishwater) that he was told was wine, and it was said that he could hypnotize birds into sitting still during his bird-watching trips. Using these stories as evidence was not far above more modern cases of saying that a suspect may have been capable of murder because he listened to Metallica, but such evidence was hardly necessary given the weight of the more tangible proof.

All through June and July, the boys' wealthy families spent a fortune on doctors who would examine the boys in hopes of finding them insane. None of this was conclusive; eighty thousand words

Leopold (right) *and Loeb* (left)
LIBRARY OF CONGRESS

of testimony on their "peculiarities" didn't really prove that the two sharp-minded boys were insane.

But they did tell a lot about what sort of relationship it was that the two of them had, and which of the two was leading the other on. Leopold had fantasies in which Loeb was the "king" and he was a "slave." Though he was the smarter of the two, Leopold had suffered from something of an inferiority complex, partly due to his sexual orientation (the nature of which was not understood at the time). The fact that he had likely been sexually abused by a governess didn't help his psychological development, either.

Both, though, were known to feel that the laws of man did not apply to them. The difference was that Leopold would say, "What is pleasant to me I have a right to do because I am an individual." Loeb would say, "What is pleasant to me I have a right to do because I am the greatest individual in society."

Leopold said he wished he had never done the deed, and that he would not do it all over again.

Loeb would have. He had felt a thrill—the one he had hoped for—when the chisel came down on Bobby Franks's head. Leopold had felt cold and empty.

It's fair to say that Leopold had put Loeb on a pedestal, at the very least. Even years later, Leopold wrote, "Dick possessed more of the truly fine qualities than almost anyone else I have ever known. Not just the superficial social graces. Those, of course, he possessed to the nth degree . . . but the more important qualities of character, too, he possessed in full measure . . . [but] there was another side. Dick just didn't have the faintest trace of conventional morality . . . I don't believe he ever, to the day of his death, felt truly remorseful for what we had done." He had only confessed, he said at the time, because Loeb had, and he wanted to stick by him.

Throughout the hot summer of 1924, the press assumed that, like so many before them, Leopold and Loeb would be pleading not guilty due to insanity. There was no doubt that they had committed the crime, after all, and being judged insane was likely to be their best shot at avoiding the gallows. The family hired Clarence Darrow, one of the most famous attorneys of the day, as the defense attorney, and it was assumed that he'd make the case that the boys should not be hanged but sent to an asylum.

Darrow, a noted opponent of the death penalty, surprised everyone by entering a guilty plea and casting aside all the evidence of insanity. He was sure that arguing the case in front of a jury would lead to a conviction, and probably a hanging; by pleading guilty, he could argue the case in front of a single judge. There would be only one man to convince to spare their lives, not a whole jury.

In court, Darrow made such a powerhouse of a speech pleading for the boys' lives that even the defendants broke down in tears (though whether they were tears of remorse or tears brought about as Darrow described, in graphic detail, what happens to a human body when it's hanged, was an open question).

The speech, combined with the fact that both boys were minors, worked as it was supposed to. Rather than sentencing them to hang in the old prison behind the courthouse, the judge sentenced both boys to life plus ninety-nine years for kidnapping and murder.

In jail, the two boys put their education to use starting a correspondence school for prisoners, and Leopold taught himself another dozen or so languages, including ancient Egyptian. He was paroled years later and lived the last years of his life in Puerto Rico.

Rumors spread that Loeb became a rapist in prison. There's never been a bit of evidence, but when prisoner James Day stabbed Loeb to death in the shower in 1936, he claimed that he had done so in self-defense when Loeb came on to him. The court ruled in his favor, despite the fact that the evidence was strongly against him. (Loeb had been slashed fifty-six times, while Day didn't get a scratch.)

The story that the killing had been in retaliation for sexual advances spread at once. In fact, on the day of his murder, the (unarchived) early edition of the *Chicago Daily News* was said to open the story by saying, "Despite his erudition, yesterday Richard Loeb ended his sentence with a proposition."

CHAPTER 22

Big Bill Thompson
The King of Corruption

When the poets write the ballad of William Hale Thompson, perhaps they will say that he was a man who had the tools for greatness—until he got involved in Chicago politics. Nearly every time I deal with a story on the historical Chicago politics, I end up aghast at what a bunch of jerks the men who've run the city have been. And Big Bill Thompson, who got into politics because someone bet fifty dollars that he wouldn't, is widely regarded as the most spectacularly corrupt mayor we ever had. He was a favorite of the Prohibition Era gangsters, which probably tells you about all you need to know about his career.

When Lloyd Wendt and Herman Kogan wrote a biography of Thompson in 1953, they opened by saying, "Once upon a time there really was a Big Bill Thompson." Less than a decade after his death, he had already become such a legendary figure that it seemed impossible that such a man had ever truly existed; even now, seeing his name on the occasional plaque at a fire station opened during his reign feels like how finding King Arthur's name on an old castle would probably feel. With all the limelight-hogging, eccentricities, and corruption of Bathhouse John, but with (arguably) more brains, William Hale Thompson was a man who seemed to have beamed into Chicago from some other reality. Other men running for office may have *joked* about staging debates with live rats standing in for their opponents, but Thompson actually *did* it.

Born in Boston, Thompson's family moved to Chicago when he was young, and a building his father owned was one of the few to survive the Great Fire in 1871, when Bill was only two years old. By the time Bill was a teenager, his father was a wealthy man with around two million dollars in real estate holdings to his name.

William Hale Thompson tries to look serious while claiming that King George V has a real conspiracy going to infiltrate American schools.
CHICAGO DAILY NEWS

But young Bill decided to throw it all away. Scraping together all the money he could, he went out west to become a cowboy. For a few years, he spent winters studying in Chicago, and the rest of his time working on western ranches. His father eventually bought him a ranch of his own to manage, and Thompson was known to his cowboys as an upright, honest man in all situations, whether he was roping steer or dealing poker.

Upon his father's death, Thompson, still in his early twenties, was forced to retire as a rancher to manage his father's business empire back in Chicago and kept his keen desire for excitement alive playing for the city football team. Though resistant to running for a spot as alderman at first, when a friend slapped fifty dollars onto a card table and said, "This money says Bill is afraid to run," Thompson scooped up the money and said, "I'll take this one myself."

Thompson became an alderman of the Second Ward, which was just about as infested with gamblers, prostitutes, and thieves as the notorious First Ward next door. Still, it was a promising start for the young man, who would work his way through the city until he became mayor. It may have started on a bet, but there was no reason not to see him as a young man who was going places.

And yet, when he was voted out of office for the last time in 1931, the *Tribune* described the reaction in the city as a sort of Mardi Gras. "Ticker tape, telephone directories torn into strips, and even firecrackers dropped from windows (in The Loop). Music blared wherever instruments could be obtained, and, where they couldn't be found, cowbells, tin pans, and any old thing provided noise. It was a celebration Chicago has not seen since the armistice." Summing up Thompson's three terms, they said "For Chicago Thompson has meant filth, corruption, obscenity, idiocy, and bankruptcy. He has given the city an international reputation for moronic buffoonery, barbaric crime, triumphant hoodlumism, unchecked graft, and a dejected citizenship. He nearly ruined the property and completely destroyed the pride of the city. He made Chicago a byword for the collapse of American civilization . . . he leaves office and goes from the city the most discredited man who ever held place in it."

This was how the *Tribune,* a staunchly Republican paper, memorialized the last Republican Mayor of Chicago.

Too much time in Chicago politics could ruin practically anyone in those days.

At the time of Thompson's election as mayor in 1915, *The Lawyer and Banker and Central Law Journal* wrote, "William Hale Thompson is a big man, mentally, morally, and physically . . . he is every inch a man of brains, of education and refinement, and, with all, aggressive to the nth degree." So, what happened to Big Bill, the promising young cowboy and hero of the Chicago Athletic Association, the man who some thought could become president of the United States?

Despite the claims of *The Lawyer and Banker and Central Law Journal* (which sounds like the most boring magazine ever published), Thompson had been elected by playing a mean game of politics, attacking Germans, Catholics, and the British whenever he felt it convenient. He pledged that he would enforce the gambling laws strictly (while promising the gamblers an "open town"). Running as a larger-than-life, bombastic character against the bland Judge Harry Olson, he was narrowly elected and proceeded to break every promise he made of giving the city a "clean" government in a matter of months.

He started out as a reformer—during the October after his spring election, he even closed all of the saloons on Sunday, forcing the local saloons to comply with a long-standing state law (which they'd quite openly violated before). Bathhouse John Coughlin published a new ballad in objection to it, but the rule held.

Still, at this point, Thompson was behaving mainly as a regular politician who just happened to have a cowboy's mouth and energy. What began to lead him down the dark path was his desire to become a United States senator, and, eventually, president. In the course of distinguishing himself, he found it made headlines to oppose American involvement in World War I. Soon, he had reinvented himself as the "America First" candidate.

But amidst accusations of corruption and other scandals, he was defeated when he ran for a third term in 1921 by William Dever, who ran on a "decency" platform. Dever was supported, veteran reporter James Doherty wrote, "by such exponents of decency as Bathhouse John Coughlin and Hinky Dink Kenna." By this time Prohibition had become the law of the land, and the Chicago underworld was growing in power rapidly. There would be little sign of decency under Dever's administration, hard though Dever tried.

Sometimes being out of office changes a politician. After leaving the presidency in 1909, Teddy Roosevelt went on an African safari and came back significantly more liberal than he had been before. Perhaps taking a cue from how Roosevelt's name had stayed in the headlines after he returned to private life, when Big Bill left office in 1923, following two terms plagued by accusations of corruption and graft, he announced that he, too, would go on an expedition: He would sail to South America in search of a mysterious breed of tree-climbing fish.

The "expedition" never got past New Orleans, but it kept Bill's name in the papers, and when he got back to town, determined to recapture the office of mayor, he had stepped up his isolationist rhetoric a notch—and let it take a rather bizarre turn.

After announcing his candidacy in 1926, he staged a bizarre debate where he argued with two caged rats that his aides had caught at the stockyards—one was named Doctor John Dill Robertson, after one of his future opponents. "This one is Doc," said Thompson. "I can tell him because he hadn't had a bath in twenty years until we washed him yesterday." The other rat was named for Fred Lundin, a former friend of Thompson's who had turned on him in graft trials.

While the audience sat, confused, Thompson lectured the rats about the evils of the man he'd identified as America's biggest enemy: King George V of England.

Thompson had found that anti-British talk played well in German and Irish neighborhoods. By way of opening an attack against Dever, he began going after William McAndrew, the superintendent of schools that Dever had brought in. McAndrew, said Thompson, was forcing schools to purchase history books that were pro-British and anti-American.

As the campaign progressed, Thompson's anti-British talk began to revolve around King George V, the then-sitting monarch, who, Thompson alleged, was bankrolling McAndrew as part of a plot to take over the United States. At various times, he even challenged the king to a fight. "Let King George try to come here and run Chicago," he bellowed. "I'll bust him one on the snoot!"

All of these ridiculous theatrics went over well in some quarters. So did Thompson's claim that Dr. John Robertson, a third candidate in the race, hadn't taken a bath in twenty years. When the votes were counted, Thompson had beaten Dever and crushed Robertson. Rumors circulated through London that a gang of three thousand Chicago hoodlums was being raised to invade England. Thompson did little to discourage the rumors.

As promised, his first act was to fire McAndrew, but in order to terminate his four-year contract, which had a year to go, Big Bill had to prove that McAndrew was a "traitor." One of Thompson's cronies wrote a report "proving" that the schools and libraries were full of pro-British materials, but it came to be known that the crony in question hadn't actually read a single one of the books. "Any intelligent person," the *Tribune* wrote, "knows that [Thompson's charge] is untrue . . . the mayor of Chicago is nothing if not ambitious, but in this he seems to take himself far too seriously."

Ambitious he was—Thompson seriously believed that he might be nominated for president by the Republican Party in 1928. But by this time, he had plenty of other things he should have been worrying about: The great gang war was in full swing—and Thompson was a favorite of both the North and South Side gangs. Rumor had it that Al Capone had a portrait of Thompson hanging up in his office, and that he had contributed over a quarter of a million dollars to Thompson's campaign. Thompson had broadly hinted that he would have a "wide open town" and reopen some of the illegal speakeasies that had been closed down during the Dever administration.

In 1928, shortly after Thompson retook the office, there was a primary election for offices of the senate and governor, as well as several lower-level offices in the "machine." The Republican Party was deeply divided between those loyal to Thompson and those who hated his guts and thought he was doing nothing to stop crime.

If he was stopping crime, it sure wasn't evident during the primary, which was marred by gang-related violence. "Diamond Joe" Espositio, Republican committeeman for the Twenty-Fifth Ward, was shot and killed near his home. A bomb went off at Senator Deneen's South Side home. Both men were in the anti-Thompson camp.

All through his third term, Thompson lived as lavishly as the gangsters. He had a masseur who traveled with him, along with a "minstrel" he had hired to write songs about him, a private cook, a tailor, and a huge assortment of goons and hangers-on. He conducted as much business as possible from his room at the Sherman Hotel—while wearing a bathrobe and cowboy hat.

By the next election in 1931, Chicago was sick of the corruption and the crime and the grandstanding. Though no one seemed to think Prohibition would be around much longer, gangland killings were on the rise, and after the St. Valentine's Day Massacre in 1929, when several members of the North Side gang, then run by Bugs Moran, were lined up and executed in a Clark Street garage, no one thought of the gangsters as Robin Hood–type characters any more. On election day, Thompson was dealt the biggest defeat in city history by A. J. Cermak—he carried only five of the fifty wards, and at least two of those were gang controlled. "The repudiation of Thompson was so decisive, so complete," wrote the jubilant *Tribune*, ". . . messages were coming in from all parts of the country and from foreign capitals saying that Chicago had redeemed itself.

"There were always those who said that Thompson wasn't really all that corrupt himself—he was just fairly incompetent, powerless to stop the gangsters or graft that plagued his administration. But after his death, safes in his house were found containing roughly $1.5 million in cash. The source of the loot was unknown, but Chicagoans had plenty of theories, and none was that it was simply money he'd saved up from wise investments.

Looking back on the Thompson era only a few years later, Chicagoans as a whole seemed to shake their heads, wondering if the whole thing had just been a weird dream. "In his time and in his way," wrote James Doherty, "Big Bill Thompson was symbolic of an era. And what an era . . . His policy of a wide-open town helped to make Chicago internationally known for wickedness. Thompson was a buffoon, a smart showman, [and] a shrewd politician, all in one."

CHAPTER 23

Dean O'Banion
Assassin, Hijacker, Singing Waiter, and Florist to the Mob

Like Kitty Adams, Prohibition Era gangsters were known to attack horses, not just people. When "Samoots" Amatuna was dissatisfied with how his silk shirts came back from the laundry, he ran down the street and shot the laundryman's horse to death.

And when "Nails" Morton was kicked to death by a horse in Lincoln Park, Louis Alterie, a member of his crew, rented the horse and "bumped it off."

Both men would eventually be shot to death themselves. The gangsters who ran Chicago in the Prohibition Era were not pleasant people to be around. There was nothing romantic about their lives.

But we've always had a tendency to think there was.

In a remarkable 1924 article entitled "O'BANION GANG LIKE PIRATES OF OLDEN DAYS," the *Tribune* wrote, "For some fifteen years, Chicago's underworld has been a gun-slinging, death-dealing land comparable to the Spanish Main and its swashbuckling pirates. Killers have lived a bloody, romantic life smacking of cutlass in teeth and daggers in belt. Life by the gun and death by the gun, power through might and death by the mightier—the story has been the same always."

But even as they went to press, Dean O'Banion's corpse was on an undertaker's slab, having been shot down in the State Street flower shop where he'd worked a day job. As boss of the North Side gang, he had double-crossed Johnny Torrio, the South Side boss, with a particularly jerky trick. And he'd paid the penalty.

Gangs had always shot at each other, but O'Banion's murder was the one that would spark the great gang war that would define the world's view of Chicago for ages to come.

In a few short years, the gang scene had changed dramatically. Various loosely organized groups had fought for control of red-light districts and gambling parlors for years, but the Volstead Act, the act that outlawed the sale of alcohol in the United States, changed everything. Booze brought far, far better profits than they'd ever dreamed of. A gallon of alcohol cost a gang with its own still about a dollar to produce and sold for four to nine dollars per gallon, and a decent still could make thirty or more gallons in an hour. This adds up to half a million bucks a year from one still, and that's half a million in 1920s money—over ten million dollars today. And that was just a single still—all the best gangs had dozens of them.

Few who had pushed for Prohibition realized just what they were doing. There was hardly a story about a murder in nineteenth-century Chicago that didn't start with someone getting drunk, and it's easy to imagine why some idealists believed that getting rid of liquor would solve an awful lot of problems.

But right from the start, no one seemed to take the laws seriously. Communion wine was still legal, and sales spiked dramatically. Other wine dealers who had been forced to sell "grape concentrate" found that sales improved if they added a warning label detailing how the liquid inside could turn into wine if you weren't careful.

But easier than making your own wine was simply to drink whatever the gangsters provided at your local speakeasy. Places where you could go to get a drink were in no short supply; some even estimate that the number of places serving liquor in Chicago just about tripled (along with the price of a drink).

Of course, all of this illicit drinking brought out a lot of problems. For one thing, it made breaking the law more fun than ever and introduced a generation to the joys of lawlessness (some say society never recovered). For another, it exposed people to some awfully dangerous concoctions, as armchair chemists tried to make their own alcohol by such dubious tricks as adding embalming fluid to drinks. Bad liquor killed at least as many people as gangsters did.

Meanwhile, as Johnny Torrio and his gang took over the South Side, young Dean O'Banion made his mark on the North.

Though always referred to as "an Irishman" in the press, O'Banion was born in Illinois and moved to Chicago's Near North Side "Little Hell," a slum almost unimaginably squalid by today's standards, when he was a kid. From his youth in the gutter, he grew up to be, in veteran reporter James Doherty's words, "a big shot hoodlum [with] plenty of nerve, but . . . a little short on brains."

Certainly he wasn't as bright as Torrio, who was an organizational genius. O'Banion just had the guts to move into the organizations other people created and stake out his claim.

When the Prohibition Era began, O'Banion and his men used their guns to make names for themselves and carve out a territory consisting of a broad swath of the city's North Side. In between jobs, Dean had time to strut around town like a peacock, allowing people to think he and his men were living a romantic life, "like pirates of old."

What really made O'Banion his money was hijacking liquor from others—some said he enjoyed the thrill of the hunt more than he enjoyed the money he made from it, even though it made him an awful lot of well-armed enemies. He also made a few enemies by shooting people; O'Banion always carried at least two guns, and the chief of police would eventually estimate that O'Banion killed at least twenty-five men.

Trying to graph who was in power, who owed fealty to whom, and who was serving under whom at this point in the early 1920s tends to give people headaches. In theory, Torrio and O'Banion were in a sort of uneasy alliance—there were shootings and all, but, in theory, they were at peace, in a sort of "you-take-yours, we'll-take-ours" deal. The two of them jointly owned several breweries. Not a single person really believed these breweries were brewing non-alcoholic "near beer," which is what they told authorities, but most who cared at all could be hushed up with a few bucks or, failing that, a few shots.

Maybe it was the general lack of clarity as to who was in charge and where the lines were drawn, and maybe it was just his own recklessness, but O'Banion didn't think twice about hijacking liquor from the Torrio gang now and then. This wasn't just O'Banion being a jerk, though; it was O'Banion being an idiot. He had a good territory and was making good money. But he kept trying to expand, and he kept on hijacking, not just from Torrio himself, but from the Genna Brothers, a gang from Little Italy who had discovered a loophole in the Prohibition laws that allowed people to keep manufacturing rubbing alcohol.

The Gennas paid people all over the Near West Side to put stills in their basement for "rubbing alcohol," and wound up with quite a supply of liquor. This not only motivated them to move into O'Banion's territory simply to deal with the surplus, it also gave them product for O'Banion to hijack. This caused a lot of tension—only Torrio's word kept them from killing O'Banion.

But the jerkiest move O'Banion made, and the one that sparked the gang war, came in spring of 1924.

In O'Banion's old Little Hell neighborhood, he and Torrio had leased the old Sieben's Brewery. Like other breweries, the Sieben family had been faced with a tough decision—either to shut down or lease out their brewery to someone else. They had leased out their operation to something called The George Frank Brewing Company. On paper, this was a company dedicated to brewing non-alcoholic beer. In practice, O'Banion and Torrio co-owned it. It was one of a number of breweries that the two of them were operating.

Owning a brewery in those days required a lot of police contacts, and both men had plenty of them. Plenty of police officers themselves thought the Prohibition laws were ridiculous, so they were only too happy to take the bribes to ignore them. But in May of 1924, O'Banion got word that there was going to be a *big* raid, a *real* raid, on the Sieben's brewery.

O'Banion got in touch with Johnny Torrio and said he was done with being a gangster—he wanted out, and he offered to sell his interests to Torrio for five hundred thousand dollars. Torrio was thrilled, paid O'Banion in full, and arranged to meet up with him to deal with the last shipment of his career.

The meeting was set for May 19, 1924, at the Sieben Brewery. Shortly after they arrived, the police raided the place, taking two hundred barrels of beer that was certainly not non-alcoholic (though, at only 4 percent alcohol, it was not particularly hard stuff), and a little black book that contained the names of six policemen, with an amount of money listed after each name. Torrio and O'Banion were both arrested, along with twenty-nine others.

But for O'Banion, it was a first offense, which meant that he was facing a slap on the wrist. Torrio, who had been caught before, was facing jail time.

From this moment on, O'Banion was as good as dead. Torrio wasn't about to keep ordering the Genna Brothers to let O'Banion live now that Torrio had been so badly double-crossed.

The fact that O'Banion had once been overheard to say, "To hell with them Sicilians" within earshot of the Genna Brothers, who were Sicilian themselves, hadn't really endeared him to them, either. But the fact that they were Sicilian had actually been O'Banion's saving grace. In the endlessly complicated branches of power, Torrio and the Genna Brothers both tended to defer to the wishes of a man named Mike Merlo, head of the Unione Siciliana. On the surface, this organization had always just been an organization for the welfare of Sicilian immigrants. But it was also a front for the mob, and Merlo wielded considerable influence. You didn't want the fifteen-thousand-member organization after you.

Torrio and the Gennas asked Merlo, whose honorary title was Don Miguel Merlo, to authorize a hit on O'Banion, but Merlo simply didn't care much for violence and kept on refusing. Such a murder would be bad for business.

But on November 8, 1924, not quite five months after the Sieben's raid, Merlo died of cancer.

By this time, O'Banion was working a day job at Schofield's Flower Shop, the State Street flower shop that he owned an interest in. This was a useful job for O'Banion for two reasons: For one thing, he very good at creating floral arrangements; for another, gangsters spent lavishly on flowers for funerals. It was not unusual for gangs who had lost a member in the latest dust-up to put in orders at Schofield's for thousands of dollars worth of flowers. When Merlo died, something along the lines of one hundred thousand dollars worth of flowers were bought—largely from Schofield's—including a fourteen-foot-tall effigy.

Two days after Merlo's death, three men entered the flower shop. O'Banion cheerfully said, "Hello, boys! You from Mike Merlo's?"

One of the men shook his hand, then pulled back on it, knocking O'Banion off balance, and the other two men fired six shots into him. He never had a chance to reach for one of the three guns that he kept in his custom-made suit.

Though many gangsters had had lavish funerals before, thirty-two-year-old Dean O'Banion's was one that Chicago would remember—and that would set the standard for how gangsters were taken down. When you shot a guy, you were still expected to see to it that he went out in style. A silver-and-bronze casket was purchased for some ten thousand dollars. Flowers filled twenty-four cars, and reporters noticed wreaths from most of O'Banion's rivals, including the Genna Brothers (who were generally known to be the killers). Thousands of people lined the streets to get a look at the procession.

Preachers criticized the whole affair. Dr. John Thompson of the Chicago Temple said, "Here is a man said to have been implicated in twenty-five murders buried with the pomp and ceremony of a king . . . Great throngs eagerly watch the spectacle and the press portray every incident in picture, cartoon, and story. What are the youth of our city to think about it?" Another preacher said, "What a tyranny we live under in Chicago!" The Cardinal refused to allow Dean to be buried in consecrated ground, though he would eventually be moved to a spot that was, a police captain lamented, only eighty feet from a bishop.

"A better boy never lived," said Schofield, Dean's partner in the flower business. "Or a squarer shooter." Schofield had met O'Banion when he was a popular singing waiter in a cafe on Erie and Clark—everyone had loved O'Banion then. Even among gangsters, it was said that no one disliked him. They might have hated his guts, but they still couldn't help but *like* the guy.

There was no violence at the funeral—just a lot of seething and loathing as the South Siders and North Siders stood side by side at O'Banion's grave.

But this was simply the calm before the storm—with a kingpin dead and Merlo out of the way, the gang war began in earnest. Over the next several months, the Genna Brothers were bumped off, one by one. They had become so unpopular that historians aren't even sure which gang killed each of them—it could have been anyone.

Three guys from the North Side jointly took O'Banion's place—Hymie Weiss, Vinnie "The Schemer" Drucci, and George "Bugs" Moran. The three of them ambushed Torrio and pumped his guts full of lead, but didn't quite kill him. Torrio was smart enough to retire and get out of town before they could finish the job.

Soon, Mount Carmel Cemetery was filling up with the bodies of gangsters. When Angelo Genna was buried, in a funeral every bit as lavish as O'Banion's, an onlooker noted that he was only a few feet from O'Banion—and Merlo and the other Gennas were nearby as well.

"When Judgment Day comes," an officer said, "and those graves open up, there's gonna be hell to pay in this cemetery."

And Mount Carmel hadn't yet received its most famous and notorious resident, the young man that Torrio had picked to inherit his empire: twenty-six-year-old Alphonse Capone.

CHAPTER 24

Al Capone

The Hoodlum Heard 'Round the World

In 2012, Vladimir Putin, newly re-elected president of Russia, was asked what he thought of President Obama's hometown.

"They say [Chicago is] good," he said. "Al Capone lived there."

For decades, Chicagoans traveling abroad have gotten much the same response when they told people the name of their town. Tell someone you're from Chicago, and they'll say, "Al Capone! Bang bang!" At various points people have also mentioned Michael Jordan or Barack Obama, but it just keeps going back to Alphonse Capone, who was described by the IRS as "without a doubt, the best advertised and most talked of gangster in the United States today." He still is.

In that same 1931 report, the IRS said that Capone had been "mentioned in connection with practically every major crime committed in Chicago within the last few years." This is the image we still have of Capone today—an immeasurably powerful young man who outwitted the cops, bought the government, and dug out a series of tunnels between buildings to evade capture. Today, there's hardly a building in Chicago that people don't say Capone used to own—or at least throw parties in.

But what Al Capone really had was a knack for PR—he was really little more than what the IRS called him: a "punk hoodlum." While his power was considerable, he only ever owned a couple of dumpy little buildings (owning more would have created a paper trail), kept a fairly low profile in the city (a lot of people wanted to kill him), and did very little to build up the industry from which the South Side gang thrived. All he really did was inherit the empire that Johnny Torrio had built.

Al Capone's mug shot. At barely thirty years of age, he could have passed for fifty.

Torrio was the real mastermind of the Chicago operation. He was the one who built up the resorts, bribed the neighbors, set up the system to purchase shuttered breweries, and truly organized all the criminals together. It was also Torrio who ordered most of the low-level gangs to quit with the bank robbing, safe cracking, and jewelry rackets, and just focus on liquor, where the profits were higher.

But Torrio himself was a man of high moral character, as gangsters go. He didn't drink himself at all, didn't smoke, and was faithful to his wife (who, in the great gangster tradition, was said to be fully ignorant of her husband's line of work). Capone lived large, and it showed in his face. At the age of twenty-five, he looked closer to fifty.

The Naples-born Capone grew up in Brooklyn and came to Chicago in 1920 as a protégé of Torrio, who set him up as the bouncer, and eventually the manager, of The Four Deuces, a four-story joint at 2222 South Wabash. There was a saloon on the first floor, offices on the second, gambling on the third, and a brothel on the fourth. Capone already had a reputation for violence—and a trademark scar on his face that served as a reminder to anyone who messed with him that he was not afraid to fight. When they called him "Scarface," Capone would occasionally claim that it was a World War I wound, but the truth is that the scar was the result of a street fight.

Torrio was the one who taught Capone to behave—the subtle difference between saying, "Are you looking for trouble?" and "We don't want any trouble." Knowing these subtleties probably saved his life on many occasions.

But when George "Bugs" Moran, Vinnie "The Schemer" Drucci, and Hymie Weiss, three notorious North Side gunmen, tried to avenge the death of O'Banion by shooting up Johnny Torrio, Torrio smartly decided to retire and get out of Chicago while the getting was good and turned the operations over to Capone, who immediately took steps for his own protection.

Even having bodyguards didn't make him completely safe; shortly after coming into power, the North Siders fired a veritable spray of bullets into Capone's car; he was spared only by being inside a nearby restaurant, not the car, at the time. Thereafter, he traveled in bulletproof cars and never went anywhere without his bodyguards, whom he paid a hundred dollars a week, in addition to various perks. In the middle of the 1920s, Capone, still in his mid-twenties himself, estimated that he was paying upward of two hundred thousand dollars a year for his own personal protection. But he could afford it; the syndicate was reportedly pulling in twenty-five million bucks annually. His reported gambling losses of more than seven million dollars weren't enough to hurt him in any noticeable way.

Though he may have only inherited the empire, and lacked the brains and discipline that would have been necessary to build it up himself, Capone was a shrewd leader, adept at covering his tracks. He held no bank account and, as of 1931, could only be found to have endorsed one check in his life. All of his dealings were done in ways that left no paper trail; when he and his gangs took up entire floors at the Lexington Hotel, they paid in cash.

So good was Capone at covering his tracks that the papers didn't even seem to know exactly what his name was. As late as 1926 the papers still regularly referred to him as "Al Caponi" when they weren't calling him "Al Brown," which is what it said on his business cards.

At that time, he set up his headquarters in Cicero, out in the west suburbs, where he ran his operations out of the Hawthorne Hotel. From his seat there, he directed the building of new saloons and brothels throughout the South and West Sides—one of the bigger ones in Stickney had sixty women working in it. Any time reformers moved in, they'd just move things to another building in another town. But this wasn't necessary all that often, because Capone was better than anyone else at bribing the police. It soon became well established how much cash a cop or politician could expect to look the other way when a beer truck went by. Sometimes Capone's trucks would travel around in a convoy with police cars for protection. But no number of body guards or police could truly keep Capone safe from the North Siders, and he took to spending as little time in Chicago as was absolutely necessary. He spent as much time as he could in Florida.

That was where he was on the day of the St. Valentine's Day Massacre, the most famous event in Chicago gangland history.

By that time, most of the big bosses were dead or retired. Hymie Weiss had been killed in front of Holy Name Cathedral on Chicago Avenue, right across the street from Schofield's Flower Shop, where O'Banion, his old boss, got the "Chicago Handshake." Vinnie "The Schemer" Drucci had been killed by a police officer while being driven over the Clark Street Bridge—no one quite believed the cop's story that it had all been a case of self-defense, but everyone was so glad to be rid of Drucci that no one really questioned it. The only kingpin left on the North Side was George "Bugs" Moran. He and Capone had gone back and forth trying to kill each other for years.

On Valentine's Day, 1929, five guys from the Moran gang (plus two guys who just thought it was cool to hang out with gangsters) had gathered in the SMC Cartage Company, a little garage on North Clark Street, to await a liquor shipment. At 10:30 in the morning, a police car drove up and four men got out and entered the garage—two dressed as cops, two in plain clothes.

Moran, for his part, was just making his way to the garage, but he saw the police car pull up and decided to duck into a nearby coffee shop, thinking that there was a regular liquor raid going on. A little raid was nothing he couldn't handle.

At this point, the details of what went on in the garage get a little hazy. We know that the seven men were lined up facing the north wall, and can imagine that perhaps one of them said something like, "All right—which one of you mugs is Bugs Moran?"

None of them *was* Bugs Moran, so no one said anything.

In response, the shooters mowed down all seven of them. At that point the two guys dressed as cops marched the two guys in plain clothes out at gunpoint, so any passing onlooker would have thought it was just a regular liquor raid.

Five of the guys were probably dead before they hit the ground. Two others were able to crawl around a bit, including Francis Gusenberg, one of the most notorious hit men of the North Side.

When the police—the real ones—arrived, they recognized Gusenberg right away and realized that he was their best chance at finding out who the shooters were.

"Frank!" they shouted. "Who did this to you? Who shot you?"

But Gusenberg was a gangster right to the end—squealing was not tolerated.

"Shot me?" he asked. "Nobody shot me."

Shortly thereafter, he died of having been shot.

To this day, no one really knows who the shooters were. Most of the local gangsters suspected that it was "Machine Gun" Jack McGurn, one of Capone's favorite hit men. More common theories today are that Capone brought in gangsters from Detroit or Missouri to handle things—the latest theory to go around is that

Capone had nothing to do with it, and that the real killer had just been a guy with a vendetta against the Gusenberg brothers, who had killed his cousin (who was, himself, the son of a cop). According to this theory, the dead man's father had helped his nephew avenge the death by providing the police car and uniforms.

But most have assumed that Bugs Moran was right: When asked, he supposedly said, "the only guy who kills people like that is Al Capone."

And it was known that twenty minutes before the shooting, a mysterious call was placed to Capone's Florida headquarters from the lobby of the Congress Hotel. Another was placed from the same location twenty minutes afterward.

By this time, Capone's own days as a gunman were probably behind him, but a brute show of force now and then was still necessary. The massacre was effectively the end of Moran's career, and the North Siders were never again a major factor in the city's underworld, but Capone still had plenty of enemies coming after him.

According to Capone biographer Laurence Bergreen, Capone had to return from Florida that spring, against his better judgment, when rumors went around that people were plotting to kill him.

The two main plotters where Joseph "Hop Toad" Guinta and John Scalise. Scalise was an old Genna Brothers crony and prime suspect for the killing of O'Banion, who now worked for Capone when he wasn't doing time in prison. At one point Hymie Weiss had offered peace in the city if Capone allowed him to kill Scalise and his then-partner, Albert Anselmi, another prime suspect in O'Banion's murder. Capone refused—and two weeks later Weiss was gunned down.

Scalise was arrested after the St. Valentine's Day Massacre, but released due to a lack of evidence. Around that time, he became vice president of the still-influential Unione Siciliana, which was now hopelessly tied up in mob issues. Hop Toad Guinta had become president after the previous president had been murdered. The fact that Capone was not Sicilian himself did not sit well with everyone in the union. Capone had always worked hard to keep the Unione on his side, but loyalties within the group ran deep, and Scalise apparently began to be swayed against Capone by Guinta.

With Anselmi and Guinta, Scalise began to plot to murder Al Capone. And when their brutally murdered bodies were found by the side of the road in Indiana, a legend spread that Al Capone had done the deed—with a baseball bat.

Exactly what had happened will never truly be known, but legend has it that Frankie Rio, Capone's bodyguard, had gotten wind of the plot, and Capone had decided to come back to town to see if it was true. With Rio, he laid a trap for them. At one of his more public dinners, Capone began to argue with Rio, and Rio slapped him in the face and stormed out—a seemingly bold move. It was all actually a ruse, though, to see how Scalise and Anselmi, who were present, would react.

And they took the bait—the two met with Rio the next day and offered to get him in on the plot to kill Capone and take control of his lucrative empire.

Once Rio passed enough word back to Capone to confirm all of the worst rumors he'd heard, Capone announced that he was throwing a banquet to honor Anselmi, Scalise, and Guinta in Hammond, Indiana. If anyone suspected that the across-state-lines meeting place was a sign of danger, it wasn't enough of one for them to stay away. After all, skipping out on a banquet when Capone requested your presence would have been a sign of disloyalty.

Nearly a hundred people were said to show up for the rich banquet, at which the men stuffed themselves. "Seldom," wrote Capone biographer John Kobler, "had the three guests sat down to a feast so lavish. Their dark Sicilian faces were flushed as they gorged on the rich, pungent food, washing it down with liters of red wine. At the head of the table Capone, his big white teeth flashing in an ear-to-ear grin, oozing affability, proposed toast after toast to the trio."

But late in the night, when the men were loopy and exhausted from all the food and drink, Capone, the smile gone from his face, stood up and glared at the men. "Did you think I didn't know?" he charged.

Capone's bodyguards fell on the men and tied them to their chairs. When they looked up, Capone was holding a baseball bat with both hands. One by one, he went down the line, brutally beating each man, busting every bone above the chest and smashing in their skulls before his bodyguards pulled out their guns and blew each man away.

When the bodies were brought home to Chicago, physician Francis McNamara, who had been working in the jail for thirty years, said he'd never seen bodies so disfigured.

Some denied, and continue to deny, that Capone was even present at the killing, or that he was capable of such an act of brutality. But, as with the killing of Colosimo, the sheer rumor that he was involved kept everyone else in line. Who would dare to plot against a guy who might beat you to death with a bat after dessert?

But by this time, a net was starting to close in around Capone. After the St. Valentine's Day Massacre, people were done thinking of the gangsters as romantic figures "like the pirates of old." And there was a new president in office. Herbert Hoover's failure to halt the Great Depression and his subsequent unpopularity makes it hard to imagine now, but Hoover was swept into office in a landslide; his work to keep Europe from starving in the early days after World War I made him one of the most respected men in the world. Though he was known to insist that the mafia did not exist, he also believed that getting Capone behind bars would show everyone that he intended to be tough on crime.

In March, two months before the brutalized bodies of Scalise and his co-conspirators were found, Hoover met at the White House with a group from Chicago about the possibilities of taking Capone down. In his memoirs, Hoover wrote, "They gave me chapter and verse for their statement that Chicago was in the hands of the gangsters, that the police and magistrates were completely under their [the gangsters'] control, that the governor of the state was futile, that the federal government was the only force by which the city's ability to govern itself could be restored." Certainly they couldn't rely on help from the mayor; everyone knew that Big Bill Thompson had been elected with Capone's help and did as he was told.

Hoover didn't really think that Capone's local crimes were any of the federal government's business, but he was still eager to send a message across the country and gave the famous order: "Get Capone."

By the time of the baseball-bat killing, the machine was hard at work finding a way to get Capone and make the charge stick. But this was certainly no easy task—dealing in cash, and sending people who wouldn't dare snitch on him to do most of the dirty work, Capone had left them fairly little to work with.

Treasury Secretary Andrew Mellon was given special responsibility to get Capone, and he chose a young man named Elliot Ness to lead an elite team of Prohibition enforcers. Initially the group consisted of fifty men, but it was soon reduced to an even more elite group of eleven that came to be known as The Untouchables. The group, with all the authority of the federal government behind it, began raiding the stills and breweries that were hiding in plain sight throughout Chicago.

Capone kept up his PR moves, opening a soup kitchen that gave out free coffee and doughnuts to unemployed men. To this day, it's common to find people in Chicago who will say, "My dad always said that if it wasn't for Capone, he never would have survived the Depression." But all of these displays of wealth and generosity backfired—it was obvious that Capone had a massive income, but he hadn't filed a tax return in years. He and his gang had been fingered for dozens, perhaps hundreds, of killings, but the tax charges were the ones that they could make stick.

In 1931, he was finally indicted for tax evasion, as well as illegal weapons possession and five thousand counts of violating the Volstead Act, the Prohibition laws. His efforts to bribe the jury were thwarted, and, though the Volstead Act charges were dropped, he was convicted on five counts of tax evasion and sentenced to eleven years in prison. The prosecutor, Dwight H. Green, later became the governor of Illinois.

For his first two years in prison, he managed to bribe his way into various privileges as he was shuffled from jail to jail. Photographs of his jail cells show fancy chairs, decorative lamps, and a fine desk. Eventually, he was transferred to Alcatraz, where he was probably the only prisoner present who was in jail strictly for tax evasion.

Capone, by many accounts, had trouble adjusting to life in the notorious prison. According to legend, early in his stay he tried to cut in line for the barber's chair. When challenged by another prisoner, he said, "Don't you know who I am?"

The prisoner grabbed a pair of scissors. "Yeah," he said. "I know who you are. And if you don't get to the back of the line, I'm gonna know who you *were,* too."

He occasionally made the news while in prison, such as when he asked to be released for two weeks so that he could use his underworld connections to find the Lindbergh baby. Authorities were not nearly so dumb as to let him out, though.

Around Chicago, his top lieutenants continued to fall.

"Machine Gun" Jack McGurn fell on hard times and took to doing low-rent hits just to pay the bills. In the early 1930s, he began to receive valentines in the mail, presumably from gangsters who believed him to be the shooter from the St. Valentine's Day Massacre. His friends took him out bowling one morning, and in the middle of the game a few men in overcoats came in and gunned McGurn down. At his feet, they left a valentine reading:

> You've lost your job, you've lost your dough
> Your jewels and cars and handsome houses!
> But things could still be worse, you know
> at least you haven't lost your trousers.

Capone's luck ran out while he was in prison. His empire began to crumble as Prohibition laws were repealed, depriving the gang of their most notable source of income. At the same time, his own brain was being ravaged by syphilis and he became noted for paranoid ramblings. Rumors continued to swirl around Chicago that he was returning to Florida at the time of his release in 1939, but he was really in no shape to handle the business any more. A doctor who examined him said that he had the mentality of a twelve-year-old. When asked if Capone was coming back, his former business manager, Jake Guzik, was even bold enough to tell reporters, "Al is nuttier than a fruitcake."

Capone never set foot in Chicago again and died shortly after suffering a stroke at his Florida estate in 1947, a shell of his former self.

CHAPTER 25

John Dillinger and Anna Sage
Seeing Red at the Biograph

Manhattan Melodrama is a pretty dumb movie. It opens with Mickey Rooney's parents dying in a boat wreck, leading to a long shot of Mickey Rooney crying that he's an orphan now. A minute later, he's adopted by an old man, who is promptly trampled to death by a horse at a political rally, leading to *another* long shot of Mickey Rooney crying that he's an orphan now. To bum a phrase from Oscar Wilde, you would have to have a heart of stone to watch this thing and not laugh.

This was the movie that John Dillinger attended at the Biograph Theatre on Lincoln Avenue in the last hours of his life, accompanied by a young divorcee named Polly Hamilton and a mysterious "woman in red" who had betrayed his trust and given him up to the FBI. They were lying in wait for Dillinger outside of the theater and chased him into the nearby alley, where he was shot to death.

In 1934, John Dillinger was the most popular bank robber in the world, and his antics had captured the imagination of a generation raised on stories of outlaws and bandits. The automobile era had revolutionized the bank-robbing industry, and the term "getaway car" had just been coined. There was no way to guess where he might strike next. Dillinger could rob a bank in one state on one day, and then rob another one a time zone away the next.

All of this coincided with the Great Depression, an era when banks were remarkably unpopular. In those pre-FDIC days, when the banks failed (as they often did at the time), they took people's life savings with them. A modern equivalent of the way people thought of Dillinger, perhaps, would be a guy wandering around Wall Street creaming executives in the face with a pie. Millions of Americans would think he was fighting *their* fight. And when

Dillinger's mug shot
LIBRARY OF CONGRESS

stories circulated that he'd broken out of prison using a "gun" that was really a block of wood blackened with shoe polish (and that, in pictures, looks as though it wouldn't fool a blind man) and had been polite to the police officers he kidnapped in the process, people spoke of him as a crafty gentleman outlaw that they'd like to have a beer with (now that they were allowed to drink again). That he was noted for his skills on the baseball field didn't hurt him, either.

But he wasn't just hitting people in the face with pies. There were also about twenty violent deaths that could be attributed to him and his friends. He wasn't robbing from the rich to give to the poor or to make any real point—he was really just another bank robber.

Of course, when a bank robber starts to become a folk hero, the FBI makes it their business to take him down fast. The FBI was a newer operation in those days and wasn't necessarily the crack team of investigators they're known as today. One historian described the 1934 version of the bureau as a team of "legal geeks."

The FBI's g-man in Chicago at the time was Melvin G. Purvis, a man who may have had the dorkiest name in history, but who always got his man (and had a knack for publicity). It was in the steaming hot summer of 1934 that Purvis came into contact with Anna Sage, whom history would remember as "The Woman in Red."

Anna Sage, then forty-three years old, was in a world of trouble of her own—she was an illegal alien who had been convicted of being an "alien operator of disorderly houses," which was a polite way of saying that she was running a brothel. She lived at 2420 North Halsted, just around the corner from the Biograph Theatre, and ran a "hotel" on Sheffield, close enough to Wrigley Field that patrons could probably hear the crowd cheering. (I've always liked to imagine the cheers rising up at appropriate times during the patron's nights with her "employees.")

Dillinger is thought to have roomed at Sage's Halsted Street apartment for the last few weeks of his life, making nightly journeys to pick Polly up at the North Side restaurant where she worked as a waitress. The last few weeks of his life, the *Tribune* said, were "gay weeks, filled with beer parties and jaunts to night clubs and movies, according to the stories told by Mrs. Sage. Dillinger, she said, posed as Jim Lawrence, a Board of Trade clerk, and spent money easily if not lavishly."

Living like this did not exactly make Dillinger, Public Enemy No. 1, a model of discretion. Polly's co-workers even joked with her that her new boyfriend looked an awful lot like John Dillinger.

And Sage knew that having access to Dillinger gave her a trump card in her dealings with the government. According to the stories, she told Purvis that if they'd let her stay in the United States, she'd lead Dillinger to them. Purvis agreed to the deal, and Sage said that she and Polly would take him to see a movie at the Biograph Theatre, and that she'd wear a red dress so that she could be identified, despite the fact that he'd recently had plastic surgery to lift his face and fill in his scars, and his trademark red hair and mustache had been dyed black.

Or, anyway, that was the way that Purvis told the story.

Purvis and ten of his men, plus five Chicago cops, posted themselves at every exit of the theater, and Purvis was waiting outside when Dillinger emerged. "It was a good job the surgeon did," Purvis said, "but I knew him the minute I saw him. You couldn't miss if you had studied that face as much as I have."

The agents swooped in and chased Dillinger down the block. He slipped into an alley that functioned as an easy shortcut back to Anna's apartment, but he barely made it past the mouth of the alley before he was shot twice in the back and once in the neck. Two women who were passing by at the time were wounded, though not seriously, by stray bullets.

Purvis's story went that he had been walking around with his coat buttoned, and somehow lost two buttons while drawing his gun. But keeping your firearms buttoned up when expecting a gunfight is not exactly crack police work, and keeping your coat buttoned on a day when the high temperature was 101 degrees is an odd thing to do in the first place. Indeed, the official story of

The alley where Dillinger was killed, re-dressed to look as it did in 1934 during the filming of the movie Public Enemies
PHOTO BY AUTHOR

Purvis has long been questioned—Purvis insisted that Dillinger reached for a gun, but most accounts dispute this (and the gun the FBI displayed as having belonged to Dillinger was actually manufactured after his death). Some even doubt that it was really Dillinger who was killed, and not a fall guy. Most now seem to assume that it was no shoot-out, as Purvis claimed, but a straight-up assassination.

But many of the crowd noted that when Dillinger exited the theater, he was accompanied by a "woman in red," who fell back behind Dillinger as he exited and raised a handkerchief into the air, then disappeared.

Sage, in her version of the story, ran right past Dillinger's corpse down the alley to her apartment, along with Polly, where she shed her red dress, put on something less eye-catching, and went back to join the crowd outside of the theater. Polly went to her restaurant in an exasperated state and announced, "Dillinger was just killed. Wait till the papers come out and you'll see."

Police immediately went to work discrediting the "woman in red" tale. Police Captain Timothy O'Neil denied that the "woman in red" had anything to do with the capture, and that it was information from a South Side underworld character that led to Dillinger's capture. It was, he said, "a big error to let Purvis handle the publicity."

No one, in fact, seems to have liked Melvin Purvis very much. A wiry man, only thirty years old at the time, he would eventually capture more public enemies than any FBI agents before him (in fact, his record still stands). He had already helped to capture Pretty Boy Floyd and Baby Face Nelson, two other outlaws who had become folk heroes. (Woody Guthrie even wrote a song about Floyd.) Purvis's own hunger for publicity infuriated Bureau chief J. Edgar Hoover (who may have simply been jealous, wanting the publicity for himself). He insisted that he and the Bureau alone had captured and killed Pretty Boy Floyd, with no help from the local police. (Later accounts contradicted this.)

He also may well have lied to Anna Sage. She had been promised the right to stay in the country, plus a ten-thousand-dollar reward, for betraying John Dillinger. However, she received only half of the reward in the end, and in 1936, they deported her to Romania anyway.

But the story that the information came from Sage, not some unnamed "underworld character," is probably correct. Sage was picked up at her apartment and brought in for questioning after the killing. Of course, she may have simply gone along with the story that she had betrayed Dillinger in order to get into the FBI's good graces, but Purvis backed up her story. He even said that he resigned from the FBI over the fact that the promise to her was broken.

In any case, by the time the police found her, she was already famous. Shortly after Dillinger's death, a poem was said to be chalked on the wall of the alley where he had been shot:

Stranger stop and wish me well
say a prayer for my soul in hell.
I was a good fellow, most people said
Betrayed by a woman all dressed in red.

Actually, according to many accounts, Sage was dressed in a white blouse and orange skirt. Whether the skirt simply appeared red in the dim light or if the alley poet simply couldn't find a rhyme for "orange" is only a matter of speculation.

Looking back at the case, it's hard to tell who the biggest jerk in the story was. Anna Sage betrayed Dillinger's trust. Melvin Purvis betrayed Anna Sage, and likely killed Dillinger in cold blood when he could have taken him alive (without wounding two innocent bystanders). J. Edgar Hoover was apparently so jealous of Purvis becoming famous that he actually had him demoted. (Purvis retired to practice law and write books about himself shortly thereafter.) And, of course, Dillinger was no saint himself. He had killed a couple of police officers in the course of his escapades, and any stories that he was robbing from the rich banks to give money to the poor were strictly folk tales.

The only person in the story who ever comes out looking halfway decent is Polly Hamilton, who was lured into the high life by Dillinger, and who, it was said at the time, truly believed he was just a Board of Trade clerk who had money to spend and treated her like royalty. Hamilton was already divorced at twenty-six (at a time when this was fairly shocking), and Dillinger spent lavishly on her, giving her diamond rings, sitting up with her when she was sick. He sang her love songs and took her on long walks on the beach. How much she knew of his true identity is a matter of dispute; she seems to have *suspected* that he wasn't really Jimmy Lawrence but felt that it was all worth it for the way he treated her—until the shooting confirmed her worst suspicions.

Purvis, after leaving the Bureau, accidentally shot himself to death some years later. (Some say it was a suicide, others say he accidentally shot himself in the face—the kind of mistake a guy who left his coat buttoned before a shoot-out might be prone to making.)

Polly returned to Chicago under an assumed name, married, and lived there until her death in 1969.

And some say that it really was a man named Jimmy Lawrence, not Dillinger, who was shot that day. They point to inconsistencies in Purvis's story and wonder (not unreasonably) how Dillinger, Public Enemy No. 1, could have been so riveted by the plot of *Manhattan Melodrama* that he didn't notice all of the FBI agents prowling around the theater looking for him.

In all likelihood, it was Dillinger all right—they kept him on the slab for anyone to walk up and identify, and a death mask was made that can still be studied. Though the details (right down to whether Anna was actually wearing a speck of red) may be in dispute, it seems that on that day in 1934, a whole bunch of jerks converged on a spot near the intersection of Lincoln, Fullerton, and Halsted, and one of them ended up lying in a pool of blood that was quickly mopped up by souvenir hunters with handkerchiefs. The Biograph is still standing today; the buildings around it have changed, but the alley is still there, leading to new condos on Halsted Street.

Bibliography

John Kinzie

Andreas, Alfred. *History Of Chicago Ending With The Year 1857.* Chicago: AT Andreas, 1887. Includes a lot of useful maps and information from first-hand accounts.

Currey, Josiah Seymour. *Chicago: Its History and Its Builders.* Chicago: J.S. Clark Publishing Co., 1912. The kind of book that tells you who owned the first table saw in the county.

Kinzie, Juliette. *Wau-bun.* New York: Derby and Jackson, 1856. Not exactly reliable but still essential as a portrait of life in early Chicago.

Miller, Donald L. *City of the Century.* New York: Simon and Schuster, 1996.

Harper the Drunk and Stone the Killer

The *Chicago Tribune* archives include several nineteenth-century reminiscences of Harper, Stone, and George White. The *Chicago Democrat* included a detailed account of the hanging of Stone. Others include:

Andreas, Alfred. *History Of Chicago Ending With The Year 1857.* Chicago: AT Andreas, 1887. Includes a lot of useful maps and information from first-hand accounts.

Algren, Nelson. *Chicago: City on the Make.* Chicago: University of Chicago Press, 1857.

Flinn, John Joseph. *History of the Chicago Police.* Chicago: Police Book Fund, 1887.

Martin Quinlan

"Border Ruffian Sexton Robbing Graves." *Chicago Tribune.* November 9, 1857.

Goodspeed, Weston Arthur. *History of Cook County, Illinois.* Goodspeed Historical Association, 1909.

"Recorder's Court Notes." *Chicago Tribune.* January 12, 1858.

Cap Hyman and George Trussell

Asbury, Herbert. *Gangs of Chicago.* New York: Alfred Knopf, 1950. Asbury is informal and known to take rumors at face value but was able to condense the history of Chicago's underworld like no other.

Cook, Frederick Francis. *Bygone Days of Chicago.* A.A. McClurg and Co., 1910.

"Estate of George Trussell." *Chicago Tribune.* December 7, 1866.

"The Trussell Manslaughter." *Chicago Tribune.* December 16, 1866.

"The Trussell Murder." *Chicago Tribune.* September 6, 1866.

Wilbur F. Storey

[Anonymous]. *Biographical Sketches of the Leading Men of Chicago.* Wilson and St. Clair, 1868.

Cook, Frederick Francis. *Bygone Days of Chicago.* A.A. McClurg and Co., 1910.

"Negro Soldiers." *Chicago Times.* April 20, 1863.

"Spiritualism at the White House." *Chicago Times.* June 2, 1863.

"Plots of Old Abe to Carry the Election in Illinois." *Chicago Times.* October 30, 1864.

Thomas Hines

Bernstein, Arnie. *The Hoofs and Guns of the Storm.* Lake Claremont Press, 2003.

"The Great Conspiracy: Dr. J. W. Ayer's Recollection of the Confederate Plot." *Chicago Tribune.* February 20, 1887.

Karamanski, Theodore. *Rally Round the Flag: Chicago and the Civil War.* Nelson Hall Inc., 1993.

"The Rebel Plot: Confession of Chas. Walsh." *Chicago Tribune.* November 8, 1864.

"The Rebel Raid." *Chicago Tribune.* November 8, 1864.

Marshall Field

Avrich, Paul. *The Haymarket Tragedy.* Princeton, NJ: Princeton University Press, 1986.

Becker, Stephen D. *Marshall Field III: A Biography.* University of California Press, 1964.

Green, James. *Death in the Haymarket.* New York: Anchor Books, 2007.

"Roped To Eternity." *Chicago Tribune.* November 12, 1887.

Captain George Wellington Streeter

"A Quiet Day in the Life of Captain George Wellington Streeter." *Chicago Tribune.* September 1, 1909.

"He Is a Modern Crusoe." *Chicago Tribune.* November 7, 1891.

Klatt, Wayne. *King of the Gold Coast.* Charleston, SC: The History Press, 2011.

Streeterville Collection, Chicago Public Library.

"Streeterville's 'First Citizen' Dies." *Chicago Tribune.* January 25, 1921.

H. H. Holmes

"Castle is a Tomb." *Chicago Tribune.* July 28, 1895.

"Commonwealth v Mudget alias Holmes," reprinted in *Atlantic Reporter.* St. Paul: West Publishing Co., 1908.

"The Confession of H. H. Holmes." *Philadelphia Inquirer.* April 12, 1896.

Geyer, Frank. *The Holmes-Pitezel Case.* Philadelphia: Publisher's Union, 1896. A first-hand account of the hunt to bring Holmes down by the detective who uncovered his crimes.

"Holmes Guilty of Murder." *Philadelphia Inquirer.* November 3, 1895.

George Pullman

Linsey, Almont. *The Pullman Strike.* Chicago: University of Chicago Press, 1942.

Pullman, George Mortimer. *The Strike at Pullman: Statements of President George Pullman.* No publisher named, 1896.

"Story of the Pullman Strike." *Chicago Tribune.* October 20, 1897.

Sudden Death of G. M. Pullman." *Chicago Tribune.* October 20, 1897.

Kitty Adams

"Blood from a Tooth." *Chicago Tribune.* August 6, 1894.

"It Is Goggin's Busy Day." *Chicago Tribune.* August 22, 1896.

"Goggin Hardens His Heart to Jennie." *Chicago Tribune.* August 27, 1896.

Woolridge, Clifton. *Hands Up! In the World of Crime.* Chicago: Thompson and Thomas, 1901. Woolridge refers to himself in the third person throughout in this remarkably entertaining account of the underworld in Chicago.

Adolph Luetgert

American Law Review, 1898.

"Arrest of the Sausagemaker." *Chicago Tribune.* May 18, 1897.

"Blow is Dealt." *Chicago Tribune.* September 2, 1897.

"Guilty." *Chicago Tribune.* February 10, 1898.

Loerzel, Robert. *Alchemy of Bones.* University of Illinois Press, 2003. By far the most complete information about the famous trial and its modern implications.

"Bathhouse John" Coughlin

"Coughlin To Get Kind of Funeral That He'd Wish." *Chicago Tribune.* November 12, 1938.

Johnson, Curt. *Wicked City.* Highland Park, IL: Da Capo Press, 1994. "The Story of Bathhouse John: Chicago's Fabulous First Ward Alderman." *Chicago Tribune.* May 24, 1952.

Wendt, Lloyd. *Lords of the Levee.* Evanston: Northwestern University Press, 2006.

William J. Davis

Brandt, Nat. *Chicago Death Trap.* Southern Illinois University, 2003.

"Death Trap Where Unlocked Door Might Have Saved Hundreds." *Chicago Tribune.* January 2, 1904.

Hatch, Anthony. *Tinder Box: The Iroquois Theatre Disaster.* Chicago: Academy Chicago Publishers, 2010.

"How The Fire Started Onstage: How Death Reaped its Great Harvest." *Chicago Tribune.* December 31, 1903.

Iroquois Theatre: A Souvenir Program.

Johann Hoch

"Chicago 'Bluebeard': A Man of Many Parts." *Titusville Morning Reporter.* January 27, 1905.

"Drama in the Death House: The Crimes of Johann Hoch, the Bluebeard." *Chicago Tribune.* December 13, 1936. This was an article based on several fascinating reminiscences of Frank McNamara, the physician whose name appears on Hoch's death certificate.

Hoch v People court case. *Northeastern Reporter.*

"Hock is Captured Courtin' No. 23." *Chicago Tribune.* January 31, 1905.

"Wives of Hock Found All Over." *Chicago Tribune.* February 7, 1905.

David D. Healy

Bannos, Pamela. *"Hidden Truths: An Interview with David Keene."* From her online thesis, available at http://hiddentruths.northwestern.edu.

"D. Healy as a Czar, Ignores Parliamentary Law, Whitewashing Himself." *Chicago Tribune.* August 31, 1895.

"The Dunning Investigation." *Chicago Tribune.* August 21, 1895.

"Dunning Patient Pounded to Death, Conspiracy Bared." *Chicago Tribune.* November 22, 1913.

Henderson, Harold. "A Grave Mistake." *Chicago Reader.* September 21, 1989.

Harry Spencer

"Spencer Gives New Details of Many Killings." *Chicago Examiner.* October 13, 1913.

Spencer v People, reprinted in *Northeastern Reporter.*

"Spencer's Death Sentence Upheld." *Chicago Tribune.* June 17, 1914.

"Spencer's 'Murders' Proved Dream." *Chicago Tribune.* October 7, 1913.

Charles Comiskey

Asinof, Eliot. *Eight Men Out: The Black Sox Scandal.* New York: Henry Holt and Co., 1963.

Axelson, Gustaf. *Commy: The Life Story of Charles Comiskey.* Chicago: The Reilly and Lee Co., 1919.

"Black Sox Case to be Given to Jury." *Chicago Tribune.* August 2, 1921.

"Story Fixing Comiskey in 1919, Says He Named Crooked Players." *Chicago Tribune.* October 27, 1920.

James Colosimo

Abbott, Karen. *Sin in the Second City.* New York: Random House, 2007.

Bilek, Arthur J. *The First Vice Lord: Big Jim Colosimo.* Nashville, TN: Cumberland House Publishing, 2008.

"Colosimo Slain." *Chicago Tribune.* May 12, 1920.

"The Murder of Big Jim Colosimo in His Famous Cafe. Who Killed Him? And Why?" *Chicago Tribune.* June 16, 1929.

Tillie Klimek

"Guilty is Klimek Verdict: Life in Prison for Woman as Arch-Poisoner." *Chicago Tribune.* March 13, 1923.

Kavanagh, Marcus. *The Criminal and his Allies.* Indianapolis: The Bobbs-Merrill Company, 1928. Kavanagh was the judge who presided at Tillie's trial; his lengthy memoir is largely a defense of the death penalty (which he didn't give to Tillie).

"Killing Ladies." *Chicago Tribune.* February 27, 1927. An account of the connection between beauty and acquittal among women convicted of murder in Chicago.

"Mrs. Klimek, Who Poisoned Husband in '23, Dies at 64." *Rockford Morning Star.* November 21, 1936.

"Wife Confesses Giving Poison to Her Husband." *Chicago Tribune.* October 28, 1922. For the entire last week of October and first week of November 1922, most Chicago papers had lengthy accounts of the developing story almost daily.

Richard Loeb

Baatz, Simon. *For the Thrill Of It: Leopold, Loeb and the Murder That Shocked Jazz Age Chicago.* New York: Harper Collins, 2008.

Higdon, Hal. *Leopold and Loeb: The Crime of the Century.* Champaign: University of Illinois Press, 1975.

Leopold, Nathan. *Life Plus 99 Years.* University of Minnesota Press, 1974.

Big Bill Thompson

"Cermak Elected . . . Worst Defeat In City History for Thompson." *Chicago Tribune.* April 8, 1931.

"Chicago Gangland: Killings Show Close Alliance with Politics." *Chicago Tribune.* March 31, 1929.

"Thompson Victor by 83,072." *Chicago Tribune.* April 6, 1927.

Wendt, Lloyd. *Big Bill of Chicago.* Evanston: Reprinted by Northwestern University Press, 2005.

Dean O'Banion

Asbury, Herbert. *Gangs of Chicago.* New York: Alfred Knopf, 1950.

"Cops Land in Jail." *Chicago Tribune.* May 20, 1924.

"O'Banion Gang Like Pirates of Olden Days." *Chicago Tribune.* November 11, 1924.

"Seize Three for Murder of O'Banion." *Chicago Tribune.* February 2, 1925.

Al Capone

Bergreen, Laurence. *Capone: The Man and the Era.* New York: Simon and Schuster, 1994.

"Capone's Life: From Barkeep to Gang Chief." *Chicago Tribune.* October 18, 1931.

"In re: Alphonse Capone." Internal Revenue Service Letter, July 8, 1931.

Kobler, John. *Capone: The Life and World of Al Capone. New* York: Da Capo Press, 1974.

"'You Can All Go Thirsty' is Big-Hearted Al's Adieu." *Chicago Tribune.* December 6, 1927.

John Dillinger and Anna Sage

Burrough, Bryan. *Public Enemies.* New York: Penguin Press, 2004.

"Clear Up Dillinger Mystery: Woman in Red is Found." *Chicago Tribune.* July 25, 1935.

"Kill Dillinger Here." *Chicago Tribune.* July 23, 1934.

"Purvis Admits Dillinger 'Deal' With Anna Sage." *Chicago Tribune.* October 1, 1935.

Index

About the Author

Adam Selzer is a tour guide, author, chief editor of the Chicago Unbelievable blog, and the boss of the Smart Aleck Staff, which produces the acclaimed Smart Aleck's Guide series. He has been featured on NPR, *Chicago Tonight, Coast to Coast AM with George Noory,* and several other outlets talking about strange stories from Chicago's history. He currently runs ghost tours for Chicago hauntings.